The Pocket Guide to Royal Scandals

Andy K. Hughes

First published in Great Britain in 2011 by
REMEMBER WHEN
An imprint of
Pen & Sword Books Ltd
47 Church Street
Barnsley
South Yorkshire
S70 2AS

ISBN 978 1 84468 090 0

A CIP catalogue record for this book is available from the British Library

Typeset by Phoenix Typesetting, Auldgirth, Dumfriesshire
Printed and bound by CPI UK

Pen & Sword Books Ltd incorporates the Imprints of Pen & Sword Aviation,
Pen & Sword Maritime, Pen & Sword Military, Wharncliffe Local History,
Pen & Sword Select, Pen & Sword Military Classics, Leo Cooper, Remember
When, Seaforth Publishing and Frontline Publishing

For a complete list of Pen & Sword titles please contact
PEN & SWORD BOOKS LIMITED
47 Church Street, Barnsley, South Yorkshire, S70 2AS, England
E-mail: enquiries@pen-and-sword.co.uk
Website: www.pen-and-sword.co.uk

WT

Please return/renew this item by the last date shown.

To renew this item, call **0845 0020777** (automated)
or visit **www.librarieswest.org.uk**

Borrower number and PIN required.

1 9 7624782 3

Contents

Contents

The Pocket Guide to Royal Scandals

Dedicated to my sister Vicky Hughes.
'The bravest person I have ever known.'

Acknowledgements

THANKS FOLKS!

There are many people whom I would like to thank, who have helped in some small or large way in putting this book together. Thanks to my agent Hilary Elston at Straight Line Management, my Mum for helping and inspiring me, (I have to keep up with the number of books she has written), my Dad David Benson for checking some facts; any errors left in are entirely mine! Others who have been supportive in many ways include Alexander Macmillan and Linda, Sue Aubertin and Bill, as well as Gwyn and Elizabeth. To my children, Kristian, Aaron, Ellis and Harry, thanks for your patience as I've been working away. Thanks also to Elmbridge Museum in Surrey, the Science Museum in Birmingham and to the staff at High Wycombe Library for overcoming technical problems for me. Thanks also to Peter and Jean Bean for the photo and to Dan Fox for artwork and I.T. advice as well as Dan Renshaw for historical advice.

My special thanks to the illustrator of the book: Bea Fox.

Above all, there is one person who has helped, supported, encouraged me and stood by me throughout everything, my wife and best friend, Bridget.

Andy K. Hughes

Introduction

Royal families have provided us with scandal and intrigue for hundreds of years. Even the ancient emperors of the Far East have their own interesting stories. In this book I will look at the scandalous stories attached to kings and queens of Britain, monarchs from abroad, and some of the outrageous and scandalous behaviour of some of the ancient leaders, from ancient China to the Roman Empire, from central Europe to modern day Britain.

There are stories of sexual torture, sexual depravity, weird punishments, affairs, harems, prostitutes, gambling, deceit, lies, violence, stitch-ups, cover-ups, mutilation, arrogance, greed, stupidity, bribery, madness and homosexual affairs. Some monarchs were killed in battle, others were executed; some were killed by their own family, whilst some had their life taken away in mysterious surroundings. There is plenty of scandal to be found from kings and queens around the world, and many strange stories. Actually there are many stomach churning stories. The book is based on fact and is not intended to persuade you of any monarchical or republican views, one way or the other. The scandal of modern day royals seems almost as bad as the scandals of hundreds of years ago. Some of the scandals in the book you will remember from newspaper coverage in recent years, other stories from hundreds of years ago may be new to you, but the level of scandal is often the same, or even worse. We can also ask ourselves: 'If nobody actually knows about scandalous behaviour, is it still a scandal?' I define the extremities of some of the torture methods and treatment of subjects, as scandalous as the affairs, sexual indiscretions and murders themselves.

Defining Scandal

The *Oxford Dictionary* describes 'scandal' as a disgraceful or discreditable action, or conduct leading to disgrace. It is bringing shame or dishonour, to discredit or disgrace. The word comes from the Late Greek 'skandalon', meaning the cause of moral stumbling and in

Middle English was actually spelt as 'scandle'. *Answer.com* calls it, 'a publicised incident that brings about disgrace or offends the moral sensibilities of society.' The *Cambridge Dictionary* calls it, 'an action or event that causes a public feeling of shock and strong moral disapproval.' *Dictionary.net* says, 'offense (sic) caused or experienced; reproach or reprobation called forth by what is regarded as wrong, criminal, heinous, or flagrant: opprobrium or disgrace.'

A scandal may be based on false or true allegations. We see scandals everywhere: sport, entertainment, media, politics, history and many other parts of life, both now and in the past. John B. Thompson's *Political Scandal, Power and Visibility in the Media*, argues that it refers to moral codes and values out of line with events, circumstances and actions. He argues that the ingredients of a scandal include elements of secrecy and disapproval that could in the end damage a reputation, but the word should not be used to belittle a major tragedy or make something more dramatic.

Whilst I agree with this well informed analysis of the word, I would add another angle. I see the contravention or transgression of values, the secrecy and disagreement as the fuel for the blazing fire of scandal. The spark which ignites it is the shock and surprise, when you really weren't expecting it to happen. If Queen Victoria had announced the end of her grieving period after Albert's death and her willingness to find a new partner, would the public have been as shocked over revelations she was 'seeing' her servant John Brown. I would also add 'care' to the equation. You have to care about those committing the scandal or those affected by the consequences.

There is scandal everywhere, probably amongst people you know or work with, maybe someone in your street. Every day in the newspapers you can see tales of scandal. We are surrounded by it. But when scandal hits those members of society who are meant to lead us, either monarchs or politicians, for example, it seems much more intriguing and much more amusing. Scandal is split into different themes, for example, financial scandal, sexual scandal and power scandal. These themes are often mixed up or several are addressed in each general scandal. People with too much money, too much power and too much time, or a combination of these, are prone to scandal. There are people for whom having too much money, power, fame or even free time, can eventually lead to their undoing. In addition, those who do not have to link action with consequence are also prone.

Introduction

There are two other possible ingredients to a scandal. We must consider the social position of those involved and the comparison between them. Then we should look at how the victims make it worse with the great cover up that usually backfires on them. First let's take a look at the social differences. Take for example a politician who is found in bed with a drug-snorting, lesbian call-girl, or Prince so-and-so having a fling with a republican minded, communist, Iraqi, drug dealer. The social position, reputation and relationship between the two parties concerned can form part of the scandal. The politician is supposedly the respectable, trustworthy person of power, yet he is linked to a hooker who takes drugs and the Prince who is regal and prim and proper is found to be having sex with a drug dealing anti-royal. This gives the scandal a second sting.

Then there is the great denial. This often makes the scandal reach a new level or shock. For example, it was bad enough that Bill Clinton had sexual relations with a White House intern (Monica Lewinsky). But when he admitted he'd lied after he said, 'I did not have sexual relations with that woman,' the scandal was not only his relationship with the girl, but also the fact that he'd lied to all of us. Likewise, John Profumo telling the House of Commons in 1963 that he had not had a sexual relationship with Christine Keeler, then admitting he'd lied in his resignation letter. Here the scandal was the affair AND the fact he'd lied to the House, and the nation.

We love a good scandal. Newspapers and round-the-clock news devour, digest, analyse and spit out scandal after scandal, and we soak up every last detail. This book is no different, cram packed with juicy scandalous behaviour from centuries gone by. If I could write a formula for the perfect scandal, I would sum it up by saying it is, someone well-known, doing something secretly they should not be doing, at a time they should not be doing it, probably with someone they should not be with anyway, getting something they should not have either, and to top it all off, getting caught, shocking most people, disgusting others, repulsing a few, angering many and amusing the rest. This book is not meant as an academic guide, but an entertaining and informative look into scandals past and present, some bigger than others, some with worse consequences than others, some cruel, others naughty, some funny, others rude, and some just plain shocking.

Chapter One

A Summary of Monarchs Since 1066

We now start with a list of English, (later British), Monarchs since the Norman Conquest of 1066, including dates, and in some cases details of death, tales and intrigue:

MONARCH: WILLIAM I (THE CONQUEROR)

Royal House: Norman
Dates: b.1027 d.1087
Reigned: 1066–1087
Cause of Death: Fell on the iron horn of his saddle
Remembered for: Invading England in 1066 and ordering the Domesday Book to be compiled in 1085/6
Place of Burial: Abbey of St Stephen, Caen, Normandy

MONARCH: WILLIAM II (RUFUS)

Royal House: Norman
Dates: b.1056 d.1100
Reigned: 1087–1100
Cause of Death: Killed by an arrow in the New Forest. Accident or murder? Unknown
Remembered for: His cruelty and the building of Westminster Hall
Place of Burial: Winchester cathedral

MONARCH: HENRY I

Royal House: Norman
Dates: b.1068 d.1135
Reigned: 1100–1135
Cause of Death: Food poisoning
Remembered for: Promoting law and order, and having 28

children (25 of them bastards, a record amongst English kings)

Place of Burial: Unknown

MONARCH: STEPHEN

Royal House: Norman
Dates: b.1097 d.1154
Reigned: 1135–1154
Cause of Death: A ruptured appendix
Remembered for: Sieges, battles and wars with Matilda, to try and keep his crown
Place of Burial: Unknown

MONARCH: EMPRESS MATILDA

(She got this name because her first marriage was to the Holy Roman Emperor, Henry V. She was never crowned in England but given the title Domina, or First Lady of the English, effectively queen.)

Royal House: Norman
Dates: b.1102 d.1167
Reigned: Feb.-Nov. 1141 (when Stephen was held captive)
Remembered for: Being the mother of the Plantagenet dynasty
Place of Burial: Rouen Cathedral

MONARCH: HENRY II

Royal House: Plantagenet
Dates: b.1133 d.1189
Reigned: 1154–1189
Cause of Death: A stroke
Remembered for: Taking on the power of the Church in England
Place of Burial: Fontevrault Abbey, France

MONARCH: RICHARD I (THE LIONHEART)

Royal House: Plantagenet
Dates: b.1157 d.1199
Reigned: 1189–1199
Cause of Death: Shot by an arrow in the shoulder during conflict. It turned fatally gangrenous

Remembered for: Being a great crusader
Place of Burial: Fontevrault Abbey, France

MONARCH: JOHN

Royal House: Plantaganet
Dates: b.1167 d.1216
Reigned: 1199–1216
Remembered for: Signing the Magna Carta
Cause of Death: Possibly poisoned
Place of Burial: Worcester Cathedral

MONARCH: HENRY III

Royal House: Plantaganet
Dates: b.1207 d.1272
Reigned: 1216–1272
Remembered for: His love of the arts and creating new buildings
Place of Burial: Westminster Abbey

MONARCH: EDWARD I

Royal House: Plantaganet
Dates: b.1239 d.1307
Reigned: 1272–1307
Remembered for: Pioneering the system of law courts and
Parliament
Cause of Death: Fell ill on the way to battle, and died
Place of Burial: Westminster Abbey

MONARCH: EDWARD II

Royal House: Plantaganet
Dates: b.1284 d.1327
Reigned: 1307–1327
Cause of Death: Having a red hot poker thrust up his anus by
English captors
Remembered for: Having a red hot poker thrust up his anus by
English captors! Completely losing control, law
and order
Place of Burial: Gloucester Cathedral

MONARCH: EDWARD III

Royal House: Plantagenet
Dates: b.1312 d.1377
Reigned: 1327–1377
Place of Burial: Westminster Abbey

MONARCH: RICHARD II

Royal House: Plantagenet
Dates: b.1367 d.1400
Reigned: 1377–1399
Cause of Death: Abdicated after a rebellion and mysteriously died in prison
Remembered for: Rebuilding Westminster Hall
Place of Burial: Westminster Abbey

MONARCH: HENRY IV

Royal House: Plantagenet
Dates: b.1367 d.1413
Reigned: 1399–1413
Cause of Death: Thought to be a serious form of eczema
Remembered for: Constantly putting down skirmishes, plots and rebellions
Place of Burial: Canterbury Cathedral

MONARCH: HENRY V

Royal House: Plantagenet
Dates: b.1387 d.1422
Reigned: 1413–1422
Cause of Death: Dysentery
Remembered for: Military leadership skills
Place of Burial: Westminster Abbey

MONARCH: HENRY VI

Royal House: Plantagenet
Dates: b.1421 d.1471
Reigned: 1422–1461 and 1470–1471
Cause of Death: Murdered in the Tower of London by King Edward IV
Place of Burial: St George's Chapel, Windsor

MONARCH: EDWARD IV

Royal House: Plantagenet
Dates: b.1442 d.1483
Reigned: 1461–1470 and 1471–1483
Cause of Death: Thought to be pneumonia
Remembered for: Building St George's Chapel, Windsor
Place of Burial: St George's Chapel, Windsor

MONARCH: EDWARD V

Royal House: Plantagenet
Dates: b.1470 d.1483
Reigned: April–June 1483
Cause of Death: Held prisoner as a child, with his younger brother Richard in the Tower of London by their uncle Richard Duke of Gloucester. They simply 'disappeared' and the Duke of Gloucester snatched the crown to become Richard III. The young boys became known as the 'Princes in the Tower'. Some bones were found within the grounds two hundred years later
Remembered for: Never being crowned and his probable murder by his uncle
Place of Burial: Not known, his suspected bones interred at Westminster Abbey

MONARCH: RICHARD III

Royal House: Plantagenet
Dates: b.1452 d.1485
Reigned: 1483–1485
Cause of Death: In battle against Henry Tudor, Earl of Richmond
Remembered for: Snatching the crown from his nephews when he was supposed to be their guardian
Place of Burial: Grey Friars' Abbey, Leicester, now not known

MONARCH: HENRY VII

Royal House: Tudor
Dates: b.1457 d.1509
Reigned: 1485–1509
Remembered for: Winning the War of the Roses and giving England a much need period of stability,

prosperity and peace, after years of battles and wars

Place of Burial: Westminster Abbey

MONARCH: HENRY VIII

Royal House: Tudor
Dates: b.1491 d.1547
Reigned: 1509–1547
Cause of Death: Gangrenous leg, which speeded up obesity
Remembered for: Dissolution of the monasteries, starting the Church of England, having six wives (beheading two of them), and fathering three future monarchs, Edward VI, Mary I and Elizabeth I. He is also associated with/given credit for extensions to Westminster Abbey and Hampton Court Palace. Henry VIII supposedly haunts Bisham Abbey, near Marlow, Bucks, where the England football team sometimes train
Place of Burial: St George's Chapel, Windsor

MONARCH: EDWARD VI

Royal House: Tudor
Dates: b.1537 d.1553
Reigned: 1547–1553
Cause of Death: Pulmonary tuberculosis
Remembered for: Being a strict anti-papist and for creating many grammar schools
Place of Burial: Westminster Abbey

MONARCH: LADY JANE GREY

Dates: b.1537 d.1554
Reigned: July 1553
Remembered for: Being used as a political pawn of the day, being called the Nine Days Queen and being beheaded by Mary I on 12 February 1554
Place of Burial: The Tower of London

MONARCH: MARY I

Royal House: Tudor
Dates: b.1516 d.1558
Reigned: 1553–1558
Cause of Death: Influenza
Remembered for: Executing lots of Protestants: she was a staunch Catholic
Place of Burial: Westminster Abbey

MONARCH: ELIZABETH I

Royal House: Tudor
Dates: b.1533 d.1603
Reigned: 1558–1603
Remembered for: Religious tolerance, long service as monarch and strengthening England
Place of Burial: Westminster Abbey (with her half-sister Mary I)

MONARCH: JAMES I

Royal House: Stuart
Dates: b.1566 d.1625
Reigned: 1567–1625 as James VI of Scotland and 1603–1625 as James I of England
Cause of Death: Stroke
Remembered for: Introducing the term 'Great Britain' to recognise a union of England, Scotland and Ireland
Place of Burial: Westminster Abbey

MONARCH: CHARLES I

Royal House: Stuart
Dates: b.1600 d.1649
Reigned: 1625–1649
Cause of Death: Executed
Remembered for: Only British King to be executed after a trial
Place of Burial: St George's Chapel, Windsor

A PERIOD OF NO MONARCHY

Oliver Cromwell takes over as Lord Protector, followed by his son

MONARCH: CHARLES II

Royal House: Stuart
Dates: b.1630 d.1685
Reigned: 1660–1685
Cause of Death: Fell ill suddenly, suspicions of poisoning
Remembered for: Many mistresses and 16 illegitimate children
Place of Burial: Westminster Abbey

MONARCH: JAMES II

Royal House: Stuart
Dates: b.1633 d.1701
Reigned: 1685–1688
Remembered for: Being driven into exile where he died
Place of Burial: St Germain-en-Laye, France

MONARCH: WILLIAM III

He was from the Dutch House of Orange-Nassau, with his title of Stadtholder, before being brought to Britain. He married Mary (a Stuart), the daughter of James II, the king he drove out

Dates: b.1650 d.1702
Reigned: 1689–1702
Cause of Death: Fell off his horse, resulting in complications such as pneumonia
Remembered for: A new style of monarchy, ruling jointly with his wife, and more answerable to Parliament; he was also surrounded by allegations of a homosexual affair
Place of Burial: Westminster Abbey

MONARCH: MARY II

Royal House: Stuart
Dates: b.1662 d.1694
Reigned: 1689–1694
Cause of Death: Smallpox
Remembered for: Only ever joint sovereign (with William III); she was also very popular
Place of Burial: Westminster Abbey

MONARCH: ANNE

Royal House: Stuart

Dates: b.1665 d.1714
Reigned: 1702–1714
Remembered for: Her vast waistline, and possible lesbian affairs
Place of Burial: Westminster Abbey

MONARCH: GEORGE I

Royal House: Hanover
Dates: b.1660 d.1727
Reigned: 1714–1727
Remembered for: Speaking no English, letting Parliament run things more
Place of Burial: Hanover, Germany

MONARCH: GEORGE II

Royal House: Hanover
Dates: b. 1683 d.1760
Reigned: 1727–1760
Cause of Death: Heart attack
Remembered for: Being the last English monarch to be born abroad
Place of Burial: Westminster Abbey

MONARCH: GEORGE III

Royal House: Hanover
Dates: b.1738 d.1820
Reigned: 1760–1820
Remembered for: Going completely mad; his son ruled for the last ten years of the reign
Place of Burial: St George's Chapel, Windsor

MONARCH: GEORGE IV

Royal House: Hanover
Dates: b.1762 d.1830
Reigned: 1820–1830
Remembered for: Scandalous sex parties and drinking sessions. He helped redesign parts of central London, such as Regent Street, and the major expansion of Buckingham Palace. He secretly married a Catholic widow for which Parliament made him get an annulment. He had lots of mistresses and

was responsible for the creation of Brighton Pavillion

Place of Burial: St George's Chapel, Windsor

MONARCH: WILLIAM IV

Royal House: Hanover
Dates: b.1765 d.1837
Reigned: 1830–1837
Remembered for: Opposing the Great Reform Bill of 1832 (which went through), giving the vote to the middle classes. While a few European monarchs were being swept away, his mad, eccentric ramblings, probably made people feel sorry for him
Place of Burial: St George's Chapel, Windsor

MONARCH: VICTORIA

Royal House: Hanover
Dates: b.1819 d.1901
Reigned: 1837–1901
Remembered for: Being Britain's longest serving monarch, so far, at 63 years.
Place of Burial: Frogmore, Windsor

MONARCH: EDWARD VII

Royal House: House of Saxe-Coburg-Gotha
Dates: b.1841 d.1910
Reigned: 1901–1910
Remembered for: Waiting a very long time for his mother Queen Victoria to die, so he could become king. He also had a famous appetite and a stomach to match
Place of Burial: St George's Chapel, Windsor

MONARCH: GEORGE V

Royal House: Saxe-Coburg-Gotha, later Windsor
Dates: b.1865 d.1936
Reigned: 1910–1936
Remembered for: Founding the House of Windsor
Place of Burial: St George's Chapel, Windsor

MONARCH: EDWARD VIII

Royal House: Windsor
Dates: b.1894 d.1972
Reigned: Jan-Dec 1936
Cause of Death: Cancer
Remembered for: Abdicating to marry an American divorcee, and his sympathetic Nazi views
Place of Burial: Frogmore, Windsor

MONARCH: GEORGE VI

Royal House: Windsor
Dates: b.1895 d.1952
Reigned: 1936–1952
Cause of Death: Cancer
Remembered for: Leading Britain through World War II
Place of Burial: St George's Chapel, Windsor

MONARCH: ELIZABETH II

Royal House: Windsor
Dates: b. 1926-
Reigned: 1952-
Remembered for: Amongst Britain's longest serving monarchs
Children: Charles, Anne, Andrew, Edward

Chapter Two

Scandalous Rulers Before The Fifteenth Century

Scandal is not a modern invention, not something cooked up by the Twenty-First Century paparazzi, for it would seem that man – and rulers – have always possessed the ability to shock, and in some cases disgust us all, and so we begin by taking a look at some of the earlier rulers and their scandalous behaviour, starting first with the Chinese Emperor, Ming Huang.

CHINESE EMPEROR MING HUANG
b.684 d.762 AD
Reigned: 712–756 AD

Ming Huang (meaning the Glorious Monarch) was a patron of the arts and music. Both of these developed in his royal court. Huang's real name was Hsüan Tsung. He had a harem of forty-thousand concubines. A lot of women to satisfy! Or a lot of nagging! That's forty-thousand women at his beck and call, to satisfy his every sexual need at the click of his fingers. But despite the huge choice, Yang Kuei-fei was his favourite, his son's betrothed. Diane Osen's *Royal Scandals* describes her as so irresistible that her every wish became a royal command. Stories have lasted that claim she was more beautiful than every other woman combined. Ming Huang had a favourite before Yang Kuei-fei, Mei Fei, who was replaced!

Yang Kuei Fei was a bit of an obsessive character. She was known as the Jade Beauty. She was apparently obsessed with jade, surrounding herself with jade ornaments, jewellery and objects. It is said she even slept on a jade bed. She also wanted lots of litchi nuts. Ming Huang had a small army of horseback riders whose job was to continually make the three thousand mile journey to southern China and back to get more supplies for her. The ungrateful Yang spurned the Emperor's affections and devotions by taking another lover behind his back. This caused her death.

TIBERIUS THE PERVERTED
b.42BC d.37AD
Emperor: 14AD–37AD

Time to rewind to the year AD14 when Tiberius Caesar became Emperor of the Roman Empire. It was at this time that Jesus was crucified. I decided to pick just one Roman Emperor for this book, and I have picked the one with the most outrageous behaviour of them all. Apart from crucifying Jesus Christ, which was bad enough, he led a sick sexual existence, that today would see him put behind bars for many years, or in some countries probably chemically castrated or executed.

He seemed quite a calm and decent chap in his youth and early reign, but something seemed to go terribly wrong with his state of mind later on. He settled himself down on the island of Capri. It is here that some of the world's most sordid sexual behaviour ever went on. But he was Emperor, whatever he demanded, he got. There was no disobeying him, judging him or running away from him. You would have just got on and followed orders.

He was quite plainly, a murderous, sexually dominant, perverted, paedophile. Michael Farqhuar's *A Treasury of Royal Scandals* describes him as having slimy and dangerous tendencies. On his beloved island of Capri he built himself a number of decorative and splendid pleasure palaces. What went on in these pleasure palaces was pure sexual scandal. He had his staff import, or to put it another way, people traffic, lots of young boys and girls from all the corners of his kingdom. They were brought in, against their will, to act as his personal and sexual slaves. He would pick any young girl or boy he took a fancy to and, despite their wishes, he would then use them for his own personal gratification. But it did not stop there. He would order some of the boys and girls to have sex together, or in groups, to perform in front of him and with each other. He is known for swimming with young boys between his legs. He also liked to have nude, young women to be his waitresses at his table for the night.

All of this was a big fun sexual game to this pervert, but not much fun for either the young boys or girls forced to take part in the sex games. It is unclear how young his sexual victims were, but many were definitely under age! Some had the courage to resist his sexual demands, only to suffer terrible punishment, having bones broken or getting a good whipping!

Tiberius was obsessed with torture, sometimes of the genitals, and execution as well. He would order lots of executions at once. Reports told of how bodies littered the steps of important buildings. Mourning relatives were banned from seeing the bodies of their loved ones, or from giving them a decent burial. Many were simply left to rot or were thrown into the river. He even executed members of his close family. Adults and children were no different when it came to rape, torture, whippings or executions. Although this would be scandalous by today's measures, it would not have been quite so bad back then. We have to accept that the ancient Romans and Greeks had totally different attitudes and standards when it came to sexual activity, *christianaction.org* says;

'The Roman emperors Tiberius, Nero, Galba, Hadrian, Commodus, amongst many others, were renowned for their numerous homosexual liaisons with children. Bisexuality, perversion and sexual deviance was widespread throughout the pagan culture of the Greeks and Romans.'

Pederasty was rife as well. This is an erotic relationship between an adult man and an unrelated adolescent boy. The age of consent in a particular culture is the deciding factor on crossing the line of paedophilia. Tiberius liked to watch, to do, and to force when it came to sex; age and sex of a person were often irrelevant. He made sure he was surrounded by nudity, intercourse, sexual degradation and torture. Meanwhile, the death of this very spotty and very smelly cruel dictator was unsurprisingly celebrated on the streets by thousands of people, all very much relieved that the old man had finally gone. He lived well into his seventies. Rumour has it he was not quite dead when the celebrations started, so someone smothered him to death. People were dancing in the streets, glad that their nightmare was finally over.

When examining the history of emperors like Tiberius, and indeed others of that time, one should remember some ancient cultures could be quite depraved. The Romans were keen on adultery, obscene sexual activities, public nudity, pornography on pots and vases in front of children; often with sadistic and masochistic tendencies. Some emperors were into group sex, incest, and prostitution. One had three hundred concubines and three hundred young boys to satisfy him. Paedophilia was rampant in ancient Rome and Greece. Tiberius, and many other emperors, all enjoyed perversions in what today would probably be classified as child molestation. Plays, including live sex, mutilation and bestiality on the stage, became common during the reign of some emperors.

KING ETHELBALD OF WESSEX
Keeping it in the Family
b.834 d.860
Reigned: 858–860

Ethelbald was King of the West Saxons, and was son of Ethelwulf of Wessex. After an eventful visit to Rome, Ethelbald's father brought back his latest conquest, a pretty young girl he had chosen to be his own wife. This young girl was also the daughter of the King of France. Judith was just 13 years old at the time. Some accounts actually put her at 12 years old. There followed a series of rows within the family and the danger of a civil war. So to make peace Ethelwulf let his son Ethelbald take control of Wessex. He kept Kent and other eastern parts for himself.

After the death of Ethelwulf, Ethelbald was officially crowned at Kingston-upon-Thames. However, Ethelbald surprised his followers by marrying his father's young widow Judith, who was still a teenager. In other words, quite disgustingly, he married his own step-mother. His actions certainly upset the Church, which declared the marriage as incestuous and against Church law. By now, Judith's father Charles the Bald was rather angry with events. He threatened to stick his daughter in a convent. He said it was for her own protection. The marriage was also annulled by the Church. Meanwhile, Judith had plans of her own and eloped with Baldwin, Count of Flanders. At a time when royal marriages were usually political, it is thought Ethelbald had taken his father's widow to maintain a strategic alliance with the Franks. This was something his father had always tried to do during his lifetime.

Around this time in history, wives of kings did not always take the title of 'Queen'. It is thought that Judith did take the title though. Even though Ethelbald had upset rather a lot of people, he managed to rule for a few years and was actually quite a popular king. He is documented as having a strong character about him. He died young though, about 26 or 27 years old.

EDWARD THE MARTYR
b. 962 d.978 (murdered at 15 years old)
Reigned: 975–978

This story combines an Anglo-Saxon King, an HSCB bank in Woking, a wicked stepmother, an old cutlery box and a nun with a spade. You couldn't make it up if you tried!

King Edward the Martyr was murdered at the age of 15. He was pulled from his horse and fatally stabbed at Corfe Castle in Dorset. Edward had turned away from his hunting party to take a short rest for a while. As he rode on horseback to the palace gates, his stepmother Queen Aelfthrith greeted him with an affectionate kiss. As he took refreshments, she ordered one of the guards to kill him by stabbing him in his back. He managed to ride off, but fell off his horse, and was dragged along, until either the ride or the stabbing, or both, claimed his life. It is thought his stepmother arranged his grisly end, so she could get her own son on the throne. He was buried in Wareham at first, which was intended to be his final resting place. But miracles started to happen around his bones. They were reburied at Shaftesbury Abbey. Again, this was intended as his final resting place, and he was declared a saint in 1001. When Henry VIII went on the rampage, destroying, stealing from the monasteries, fearful of losing Saint Edward's sacred bones, a nun got busy and buried them in the Abbey grounds. They stayed there until 1931 because nobody could find them. A casket with a skull and some old bones was eventually dug up, and immediately there was a legal wrangle over who owned the grisly find. During the dispute, the bones were put in a cutlery box and kept in the vault of the HSBC in Woking, in Surrey. Now the remains belong to a sect of the Russian Orthodox Church. Edward's remains lay under a new shrine, just outside Woking.

WILLIAM THE CONQUEROR
b.1027/8 d.1087
Reigned: 1066–1087
William the Conqueror

William the Conqueror overcame the stigma of being illegitimate and became Duke of Normandy. They called him William the Bastard (probably out of earshot), or *Guillaume le Bâtard* in his native tongue. This was a fearsome warrior who commanded many men, out smarted ambitious rival noblemen and members of his own family, as well as threats of rebellions and invasion. He's best known

for defeating King Harold of England at the Battle of Hasting in 1066. Part of William's life (and death) is stained by scandal. William asked Count (Baudouin) Baldwin V of Flanders for his daughter's hand in marriage. Matilda, however, was not impressed because she was in love with an Englishman. Matilda poured scorn on William's marriage proposal apparently saying she would become a nun before marrying a bastard. Besides, Princess Matilda of Flanders and William Duke of Normandy were distant cousins. This did not go down too well with William. He lost his temper and attacked Matilda as she left church. He gave her a good kicking, slapped her around, threw her to the ground and tore off some of her clothes. Despite beating up the woman he wanted to marry, he finally got her to agree to wed in 1052, at one of his castles in Normandy. The marriage was initially condemned by Pope Leo IX, a bit of a scandal in its day.

When William died in 1087, it is thought he had ruptured himself on his horse saddle. His 'burial' was a scandal too. His servants left him to rot in the desert after robbing him of his valuables.

KING WILLIAM II (RUFUS)
b. 1056 d.1100
Reigned: 1087–1100

To be assassinated is bad enough, but to be assassinated upon the orders of your own brother is even worse. It is difficult to be entirely sure this was William II's fate, but all fingers seem to point at his brother, who later became King Henry I of England. First let us look briefly at how William II came to the throne. He made many enemies, not just with his opponents, but with his family and with the Church as well. He certainly knew how to stir up a bit of trouble. But he was king and he knew he could do pretty much what he liked, or at least that is what he thought.

He was William the Conqeror's third (second surviving) and apparently favourite son. When William I died he left Normandy to the eldest son Robert, and England, which he had conquered in 1066, to Rufus. There was trouble from the start, because the powerful Norman barons in England wanted one ruler of Normandy and England combined. They did not like the idea of the territories being split into two parts. They preferred Robert, so made plans to kill Rufus. In 1088, under the command of Odo, his relative, rebellions were formed across the eastern side of England.

Rufus had a reputation for being brutal and corrupt, but got the English on his side by bribing them. He promised to cut their taxes and introduce more liberal laws. Because of this backing, the rebellion was beaten, but Rufus stupidly did not keep to his promise over the tax cuts. In 1095, another baron-led rebellion started. William was brutal and cruel when punishing the ringleaders. William enriched himself with Church money and attempted to undermine its authority by not replacing key Church figures when positions became vacant. In 1093, he chose Anselm, Abbot of Bec as the new Archbishop of Canterbury, but they constantly argued over William's authority over the Church. Anselm fled England in 1097, realising he could never get his own way over such a mean and odious king. When he had left the country, Rufus wasted no time in seizing all his lands around Canterbury.

On 2 August 1100, Rufus was out hunting in the New Forest, in Hampshire, when he was shot in the back with an arrow. He was killed. History has always suggested the assassination was carried out by a man called Walter Tyrell, but this remains a royal 'who dunnit' and a scandal that the assassination may have been carried out on the orders of his brother, perhaps, who later became King Henry I of England. This would imply a murderer and an assassin had acceded to the throne, although there is actually a lack of evidence to support this.

William's body was found by a group of peasants the following day, the nobles with him had already disappeared. His brother Henry had already headed for Winchester where he could take control of the royal treasury. Henry then went to London to be crowned. Many historians argue William was not assassinated at all. They claim Tyrell shot William by mistake, and had tried to help him, panicked and then fled.

EDWARD II
b.1284 d. 1327
Reigned: 1307–1327

Edward inherited a fairly secure throne, during a fairly peaceful time in England. But it has been argued he messed it all up. Historical writer Charles Phillips says Edward II made a series of poor judgements, both privately and publicly, which in turn led to him making real enemies with his own queen and some of the country's leading barons. It's this animosity that caused his painful downfall. This is an eye-watering story of blood, guts and torture in the extreme. There's not a man on this planet who will be able to read this section without his blood running cold, shuddering, crossing his legs, or even fainting!

There was already scandal at court during the reign of Edward's father, also called Edward. The scandal was over Edward I's son (the future Edward II) and his close friendship with a man called Piers Gaveston. It appeared to be a full on homosexual affair and Edward junior enjoyed the company of many young men. He asked his father, the then King Edward I, to bestow lands and titles on his 'friend'. A furious King banished Gaveston from England and apparently called his son a whore. But when Edward I died and his son Edward II became King, he brought back his lover from overseas and gave him lands and titles, including that of the Earl of Cornwall.

Trouble started when Edward went on a diplomatic mission to France, to try and get the French king's daughter, Isabella, to marry him. In the 1300s marriages between kings, queens, princes and princesses were not about love, they were about uniting countries and royal dynasties, forging alliances and friendships, all to help secure the dynasty and peace for the land. Mistresses were for sexual excitement and fooling around. The wife was for running the house and producing children. So it's not beyond the realms of reality that a homosexual Edward married Isabella. Back in England, Edward had left Gaveston in charge, ironically a role often reserved for the queen of the land. The barons hated this idea and revolted. Upon his return in 1311, Edward had to agree to certain demands limiting his powers and was forced to strip Gaveston of his lands, powers and titles, forcing him back into exile. Gaveston sneaked back and was caught by some of the barons in Warwickshire, where they beheaded him.

Phillips claims this was a turning point, despite Edward's grief; he argues it made him concentrate on his marriage to Queen Isabella. In 1312 they had a son, confusingly called Edward as well. In 1314 Edward II lost a major battle at Stirling Castle, besieged by Scottish forces under Robert the Bruce. Edward's defeat was serious, he was on the run, and Thomas, Earl of Lancaster, made himself ruler of England. Edward's new allies from the Welsh Marches were given lands and titles by Edward. Hugh Despenser and his son, also called Hugh, were banished by the Earl of Lancaster and Edward went to war with the Earl, defeated him in 1322, and brought back the two Hughs. Meanwhile Queen Isabella was furious over Edward's rather special and close relationship with the younger Hugh and went back to France in protest, along with the Earl of March, Roger Mortimer, and her son the future King Edward III. Mortimer was a long-time enemy of the Despenser family.

Isabella and Mortimer took up arms against Edward II, with help from an army from Flanders, and invaded England in 1326. Hugh, the younger Despenser, was captured at Hereford. He had his genitals sliced off, his entrails cut out and set alight, and was then beheaded and quartered: Isabella had got her revenge. Next Edward II was captured and imprisoned, first at Kenilworth Castle, then at Berkeley Castle in Gloucestershire. He was forced to abdicate in favour of his 14-year-old son.

Edward's guards, with unusually high spirits, rammed a metal funnel into his anus after he had failed to starve to death. The guards then got a red-hot soldering iron and thrust it deep into his bowels, creating an excruciating and very slow death. Rumours are that Edward's screams could be heard 30 miles away.

Chapter Three

Scandalous Rulers of the Fifteenth to Nineteenth Centuries

VLAD THE IMPALER
b.1431 d.1476
Ruled: 1456–1462

Vlad, 'the Impaler', as he was known, was one of the most violent, sadistic and cruel leaders in history. His methods of execution and torture would not have even crossed the minds of 99 per cent of history's sickest rulers. *vladtheimpaler.com* says 'Vlad the Impaler probably caused more rivers of blood to flow than any other ruler in the history of the world.' He had a talent for creating the most cruel type of suffering. It begs the question, how much of it was part of a severe mental problem, and how much was from his sick mind of weird sexual sadistic behaviour. Vlad was Voivodes of Walachia in modern day Romania. In the West, Vlad is best known for inspiring the name of the vampire in Bram Stoker's novel, *Dracula*.

As ruler, Vlad unleashed a wave of death and torture on enemies or anyone at home who upset him. He used many methods of execution and torture including:

- Hammering nails into the head
- Chopping off arms and legs
- Slicing off noses and ears
- Skinning, scalping and burning
- Mutilation of sexual organs
- Strangulation
- Cutting off women's breasts
- Boiling alive in a cooking pot, head stuck out through a hole in order that the screams could be heard

- Blinding, often by ramming red hot pokers into a person's eyes
- Adulterous wives had their sexual parts cut out
- Many wives had their breasts cut off, their husbands then being forced to eat them
- Young children were roasted alive and force fed to their wailing mothers
- The skinning of feet and rubbing in of salt to the wounds

IMPALEMENT

This is the method of scandalous torture and execution for which Vlad became notorious. It was his favourite past time and he got immense pleasure from it. If you were sentenced to die by being impaled, you were guaranteed a very long and very slow demise. Victims of impalement suffered for days at a time. The end result was always death, but sometimes it just took a long time to get there. Young impaled mothers often held their babies, who had also been pierced and killed.

Vlad admiring his work

A carefully oiled stake was slowly inserted into the anus or vagina, carefully positioned so as not to pierce any vital organs which would speed up death and reduce Vlad's hours of entertainment watching his victims die slowly in agony. Sometimes the executioners would pierce the victim through the stomach instead. The stake was hoisted upright and placed into the ground. The weight of the victim's own body pushed him or her down the stake. The longer or higher the stake, and the higher the victim was up in the air, symbolised a higher social rank. Nobody was exempt from this type of execution; men, women, great lords, young children were all fair game for Vlad. He was known for having hundreds of people impaled at the same time, and walking amongst the screaming victims, enjoying the spectacle and admiring the suffering and screaming.

Vlad was a vassal of the King of Hungary and the Ottoman Sultans, the latter of whom he paid off with regular payments of young boys! Eventually, Vlad lost his small empire and was imprisoned, where he resorted to impaling small creatures in his cell. Later in life he regained power, but was killed in battle against the Turks. The story of his torture became the first best-seller in European history. Estimates of the number of his victims range from forty-thousand to almost a hundred thousand, but it is the sheer cruelty that is as important as the number of deaths.

GALEAZZO MARIA SFORZA
b.1444 d.1476
Ruled: 1466–1476

He was Duke of Milan and known for being a cruel, lustful, bloodthirsty, extravagant and unforgiving despot. He was the son of Francesco Sforza and Bianca Maria Visconti. In 1466, when he was away leading a military expedition in France, his father died. Galeazzo had to get home through enemy territory, entering Milan to a great reception. At first he ruled jointly with his mother, until he decided he wanted all the power for himself and had her ousted out of the post. Despite his cruel treatment of others, especially women and opponents, he was a forward thinker in the field of canal building for irrigation, farming and commerce in general.

He had a real cruel streak to his nature. He liked to pull off the limbs of his enemies with his own hands. He didn't treat his allies much better either. He is supposed to have raped the wives and daughters of his own noblemen. He had a sadistic nature too, taking great pleasure in devising instruments of torture to use on men who had upset him. Examples of his cruelty include: making a poacher swallow a whole hare until he choked, nailing a man alive to his own coffin and leaving him to bleed and die very slowly, and starving to death a priest who had predicted his reign would be short.

Not surprisingly, Galeazzo was assassinated by three of his many enemies. High-ranking officials in the Milan court were responsible for killing the cruel duke. One was angry because Galeazzo would not take his side in a land dispute, the other was a Republican at heart, and the third accused Galeazzo of taking his sister's virginity. These three conspirators planned to attack him at church. They got him on the steps of Milan Cathedral on 26th December, 1476. The three were supported by about 30 friends. Such was the hatred for the duke that nobody broke ranks and spilled the beans: they all wanted him dead. He was stabbed in the groin and chest by one of the men. In Diane Osen's *Royal Scandals* she says the Republican conspirators spent days rehearsing the assassination by stabbing each other with protected daggers.

Galeazzo's body was dragged through the streets by a celebrating mob, beating the corpse with delight. They took it to his house and hung it upside-down on the outside, chopping off his head first. His right hand, blamed for all the sins, was cut off, burned and put on display.

THE PRINCES IN THE TOWER

EDWARD V OF ENGLAND
b.1470 d.1483?

RICHARD, DUKE OF YORK
b.1473 d.1483?

They were the only sons of Edward IV of England and Elizabeth Woodville. What happened to them remains a mystery to this day. These days it would be impossible for two princes to just vanish. But this is exactly what happened. Today this would be a scandal, with a police hunt, a possible murder inquiry and rolling news channels choking on their own excitement.

Here is what happened, as far as we know. In 1483, King Edward IV died and his heir Edward V would have been king, but he was just a child. Edward IV had left clear instructions that his brother Richard, Duke of Gloucester, should act as protector. Richard moved little Edward and his younger brother Richard to the Tower of London for their own 'safety'. Meanwhile, possibly due to political lies, Edward IV's marriage was declared void because of his alleged pre-contract to marry someone else. In those times, this type of commitment was as good as a marriage, therefore invalidating his 'second' marriage. This meant the princes in the Tower were illegitimate and therefore had no right to the throne. The Duke of Gloucester conveniently snatched the crown, becoming the next king, Richard III. But nobody knows what happened to the princes who had been taken to the tower. Common history stories suggest Richard had murdered them to stop them reclaiming the throne later on. They were last seen alive in 1483.

Historian Somerset Fry, in *Kings and Queens* argues there's no evidence Richard murdered the princes, despite detailed forensics of two boys' skeletons found in the White Tower in 1674. He points out that historian Horace Walpole (son of Robert Walpole) has written extensively on the matter and completely exonerated Richard.

Others believe when the future Henry VII defeated Richard III in battle in 1485, to take the crown into the Tudor line, he killed the two princes who were still being held captive, to stop their future claims to the throne. The other suspect was Sir James Tyrell, a servant of Richard. He apparently confessed to the murder of the princes, after being arrested for treason in 1502. James Tyrell was convicted of treason at the London Guildhall on 2nd May and executed four days later. Thomas More, a Tudor loyalist claimed Tyrell was the murderer, acting on Richard's orders, and told the story of Tyrell's so-called confession. No copy of the confession survives today.

There is no definitive proof about who killed the princes, despite several names in the picture. Their deaths were not publicly announced until 1486. Shakespeare portrayed Richard as a murderous uncle.

THE RUSSIAN TZARS AND THEIR MARITAL MEAT MARKETS

IVAN THE TERRIBLE
b. 1530 d. 1584
Reigned: 1533–1584

Best known for expanding his lands, killing his son and poisoning his wives. Some Russian tzars treated women very badly when intent on marriage and producing heirs. In the Seventeenth and Eighteenth Centuries Russian tzars scandalously sent courtiers out into the country in search of possible love mates. If they saw marriage candidates, then they would drag them back to the palace, if necessary capturing them. We are not talking about one or two victims for the Russian royals, but hundreds at a time. Ivan the Terrible's father was Vasilij III. He captured one-thousand-five-hundred girls. His son had an even bigger choice when it came to satisfying his loins.

The girls were all imprisoned together and the Tzar would examine each girl closely every morning, before throwing down a handkerchief to tell her she was out of the competition. He thought she would be disappointed at not winning his love and affections. In reality, she was probably relieved at not being selected to be road tested and allowed to go home. It was all treated like a competition, fun for the men, frightening for the girls: a bit like a reality TV programme, with a different girl being booted off every time. But this was no fun. It was a sick way to treat women, and all for the Tzar's personal pleasure. The winner of the 'competition' awaited a terrible fate. First she had to physically submit to the Tzar; then she had to give him all her sisters and other female relatives for his personal pleasure and perversion. After that, she was often shut away in all-female quarters, to lead a life of prayer and be grateful.

The tzars were a misogynistic and violent breed. In 1581 Ivan beat up his pregnant daughter-in-law, causing her to have a miscarriage. His son, also called Ivan had a huge row with his father. Ivan senior hit his son on the head, killing him. The story is told in a famous Repin painting called *Ivan the Terrible Killing his Son*. He also had two of his seven wives murdered.

Ivan the Terrible tortured and killed his opponents and was known to fly into a fit of rage at a moment's notice. As a boy, Ivan IV suffered under the regents who were meant to rule for him. The three-year-old was badly treated and tortured at home by the boyars who were fighting to come to power. He later persecuted them. He had one of the leaders, called Andrei Shuisky, fed to his dogs to show off his power.

HENRY VIII AND ALL THOSE WIVES
b.1491 d.1547
Reigned: 1509–1547

Henry nearly wasn't king at all. History almost took an entirely different course. If this had happened, we would never have known any different. Arthur, Prince of Wales, was King Henry VII's eldest son and heir to the throne. Arthur would have been the second Tudor king. He was born in 1486, but died at the age of 16, in 1502. Henry, who was to be the next Archbishop of Canterbury, was now preparing to be the next king.

Henry VIII's reign was full of scandal of one sort or another, to do with marriage, religion and succession. He came to the throne at the

Henry VIII, the most scandalous monarch?

27

age of 18, just a generation after the long and painful War of the Roses. He wanted to avoid the possibility of more war or civil unrest and knew he had to have sons to safeguard the future of the royal dynasty. This would perhaps deter the old Plantagenet supporters from causing trouble in the future, to try and get back the throne which they saw as rightfully theirs. It was this uncertainty over having sons and securing the country that would plague Henry for much of his turbulent reign. He became absolutely obsessed with having sons. It was his desire for sons that lay behind the famous divorces and executions of his wives, the dissolution of the monasteries, and the creation of the Church of England. Henry reigned during a time of great change in religion and politics. Many of the events that took place have been carefully recorded and there is an abundance of evidence about the life of Henry VIII, his advisors and his six wives. Some of the scandal in his reign was down to the treatment of and behaviour (or alleged behaviour) of some of his wives.

Here we should look at each of the six wives and what they did, were accused of, and their fate. Some of the women played a more interesting and scandalous role in Henry's life than others. Many will argue that his breaking with Rome, the destruction of monasteries, the murder of opponents and monks, were the real scandals of Henry's reign. Some think his treatment of his poor wives and others is the real scandal. The reality is that Henry's entire reign was fascinating, scandalous and eventful. He really was an unusual character, and we can feel his living history at places like Hampton Court. Unfortunately, some of his homes, even the bigger ones, have been lost over the years. The palace of Oatlands, for example, did not survive very long, and ended up being buried under a housing estate in Surrey. Tudor secrets will remain buried there for hundreds of years. Today, children learn the fate of Henry's wives by saying 'divorced, beheaded, died, divorced, beheaded, survived'. However this is technically inaccurate because the divorces were actually annulments.

CATHERINE OF ARAGON (SETTING THE SCENE)
b.1485 d.1536
Married to Henry VIII in 1509

Catherine's marriage to Henry was an unlikely event and he had diffi-culty in coming to terms with the idea of marrying his brother's widow. Meanwhile, Henry was aware that sexual relations with a brother's wife were forbidden in Leviticus 18: 1–19; while Leviticus 20: 21 warned that no children would be born to such a marriage. However, Henry married Catherine of Aragon (his first wife) just before his coronation. Twenty years of marriage to Henry had only managed to produce one healthy long-living female, Mary, the future Mary I, but no sons had survived. Several babies died very young, soon after birth. Henry VIII had to have a surviving son, to eventually succeed him. He therefore had to find a way of getting rid of his wife, who had probably become too old to bear children anymore. He decided, because Catherine had been his sister-in-law, the marriage was against Church law and it was jinxed, never to be blessed with a son.

Henry had been plotting in the background for years to get rid of his wife by divorce, without her even knowing. Political and legal wrangling continued for around six years. Catherine eventually found out and protested that she and Arthur never consummated their short marriage and therefore were not legally husband and wife. Catherine was determined to keep her position, and that of her daughter Mary. In 1533, Henry's new love, Anne Boleyn had become pregnant. Henry had still not been able to persuade the Pope to annul his marriage, despite many negotiations known as the King's Great Matter. Henry got Thomas Cranmer, the new Archbishop of Canterbury to grant the annulment through new laws. Catherine was stripped of her titles and privileges, and sent away. She was no longer Queen, and would be known as the Princess Dowager of Wales. Henry had broken from Rome and became the Head of the Church of England. Hundreds of monasteries were destroyed or confiscated, along with their riches and treasures. His daughter Mary was declared a bastard. This marriage sets the scene for more scandalous marriages to follow, although one could argue it was scandalous enough that the Queen of England, for so many years, was simply dispensed of because she bore no sons for the king and was too old to bear any more children in the future. With their marriage finally annulled, Henry was now free to marry anybody else he so wished.

In 1536, Catherine died at Kimbolton Castle. She was buried at Peterborough Abbey, which was later known as Peterborough Cathedral, after the dissolution of the monasteries. Her funeral ceremony was based on her title of Princess Dowager, something she never recognised.

ANNE BOLEYN
b.1500 or 1501 d.1536
Married to Henry VIII in 1533

Here, there are a number of different scandals to consider. Henry's beheading of his wife. Accusations she slept with many other men, and committed treason. Anne was born around 1500, and served in royal circles in both England and France. Henry VIII it seemed wanted her as his mistress at first. He had already had her sister Mary for his pleasure. Anne was determined it would be different for her. She decided it was queenship and marriage or nothing at all; take it or leave it. Henry planned to marry Anne, who was younger, to have sons, and to carry on the Tudor dynasty. A number of love letters from Henry to Anne survive in the Vatican library. In 1528, Anne appeared at the royal court and showed interest in religious reform. It is thought she had real influence over Henry and his ideas of reform. The legal debates surrounding the marriage of Henry and Catherine of Aragon dragged on and on. Anne's influence at court made her unpopular, which eventually led to her downfall. In 1533 Anne and Henry were secretly married. She was, by now, pregnant. Henry did not want his new 'son' to be illegitimate, and so hurried plans for their wedding. In autumn of that year, she gave birth to Princess Elizabeth.

The new Queen was not a popular figure. Her enemies got the King to sign a document calling for an investigation into alleged events that could result in charges of treason being made against the Queen and others. Anne was accused of sleeping with five other men, whilst married to Henry. She probably knew her days were numbered straight away. Anne's friend Mark Smeaton, who was a court musician, was arrested and tortured into making 'revelations' about Anne and declaring her guilty. After he complied, he was promptly hanged and quartered. Other arrests during the scandal included Sir Henry Norris and the Queen's own brother. On the 2nd of May 1536, Anne was arrested and told about the charges against her; incest, adultery, and plotting to murder Henry. There were more arrests after this and further charges of adultery. Several men were hung, drawn and quartered while still alive.

Anne and her brother were put on trial. More than two thousand people were there to witness the events. Anne denied all the charges and conducted herself with dignity throughout, as did her brother. There was little evidence against them, and despite the trumped up charges, they were found guilty and were executed. Anne's enemies, and there were plenty of them, had finally got their own way and turned gossip into scandal. Two days later her brother was executed on Tower Hill and the court decided another four men condemned with the Queen would be beheaded, rather than being dis-embowelled while still alive. On the 19th May, Anne was executed at 8 o'clock in the morning, in private. She made a small speech to the few people allowed in, before being blindfolded and putting her head on the block.

'Good Christian people, I am come hither to die, for according to the law, and by the law I am judged to die, and therefore I will speak nothing against it. I am come hither to accuse no man, nor to speak anything of that, whereof I am accused and condemned to die, but I pray God save the king and send him long to reign over you, for a gentler nor a more merciful prince was there never: and to me he was ever a good, a gentle and sovereign lord. And if any person will meddle of my cause, I require them to judge the best. And thus I take my leave of the world and of you all, and I heartily desire you all to pray for me. O Lord have mercy on me, to God I commend my soul. To Jesus Christ I commend my soul; Lord Jesus receive my soul.'

Just before her execution, the Queen's marriage to Henry was dissolved and declared invalid. Technically, if she had never been married to him, how could she have committed adultery? This, however, was conveniently overlooked by everyone at the time. Anne and Henry had one daughter, Elizabeth, who later became Queen Elizabeth I. She was also declared a bastard by the king. Thousands of visitors a year visit the spot where Anne was executed. The legend of Anne says she had a sixth finger and lots of beauty spots, which is probably untrue!

JANE SEYMOUR
b. about 1508 d.1537
Married to Henry VIII in 1536

Henry wasted no time after Anne's execution. Within 24 hours he and Jane Seymour were formally betrothed. They married in May. At last! A son is born. Jane gave birth to the future King Edward VI in 1537. She died 12 days later of a fever. Henry adored Jane and was absolutely devastated. Out of the six, it is interesting to note that Jane is the wife he is buried next to, at St George's Chapel in Windsor. Jane is often referred to as Henry's 'true' wife.

ANNE OF CLEVES

b.1515 d.1557

Married to Henry VIII in 1540

She was sold to Henry as a good looking girl by those around him, but he was appalled when he actually met her for himself, after he had agreed to marry her. The marriage was mainly for political reasons, to forge allies with other countries who supported church reforms. Henry's painter Hans Holbein was sent to paint a picture of Anne. When he eventually met her though, Henry called her 'a Great Flanders Mare' and 'a Dutch Cow'. He made it clear that he couldn't sleep with her because she was so ugly! He married out of duty, then soon after got the marriage annulled and gave her titles and land, and basically got rid of her. She put up no fight, and agreed the marriage had not been consummated. He did visit her though, from time to time. Her official title was 'the King's sister' and they remained on good speaking terms, and she managed to keep her head, which was the main thing. Anne lived a quiet life, causing no trouble for Henry, out in the English countryside until 1557.

KATHERINE HOWARD

b. about 1521 d.1542

Married to Henry VIII in 1540

Sixteen days after he had got rid of Anne, Henry took wife number five, Katherine Howard, in July 1540. He was 49 years old, and about 30 years older than his new wife. She had been a lady-in-waiting to Anne of Cleves and caught Henry's eye fairly quickly. Katherine's uncle, the Duke of Norfolk, no doubt encouraged her to take advantage of the King's attentions as a way of increasing his own influence over the monarch. On 28th July, Henry married Katherine in secret, at the Palace of Oatlands. He wanted it to be kept quiet from as many people as possible so he could enjoy his new bride. Henry thought she was the complete opposite to Anne of Cleves in the looks department. He was an older and overweight man and he was keen to have intimate carnal knowledge with the pretty young Katherine. He visited the bedroom of the young girl almost every night for the first few months of their marriage, so he could try and get her to conceive and have a son. Henry had a great time with the lively, sprightly Katherine and was absolutely besotted with her. He lavished so many gifts on her; ranging from diamonds to lands and property, as well as countless dresses of the fashionable French style. At this point Henry executed a number of men who had supported or arranged his marriages to other women. Katherine was no doubt enjoying the attention from all at court, and the power and the adulation. Her family were in the King's favour too, for now. It was around this period that Katherine showed kindness to certain prisoners and persuaded the king to release a number of well-known ones.

Katherine's world was to come crashing down when news broke of her boisterous and flirty past. When she lived with a group of girls (about a dozen of them or so) under the watchful eye of the Duchess of Norfolk (as Katherine's mother had died) she took part in late night parties with amongst others; Henry Mannox, a music teacher, Thomas Culpepper, and mandolin player Francis Dereham. Whether it was Katherine's stupidity, innocence or naivety that saw her mixing her dodgy past with her regal future; she invited all three of these men, into Henry's court. It was only a matter of time before rumours of liaisons started.

Dereham's over-familiar behaviour towards the Queen at court came to Henry's attention. Archbishop Thomas Cranmer was now in a difficult position because he had to decide whether or not to inform the King that his wife used to be a flirt, whore, or however he chose to see it. If the gossip turned out to be just that, malicious gossip, Cranmer knew he would be in trouble with the King. So, how do you tell a king who has a bad temper and likes to decapitate people that his beautiful young wife whom he adores, was a bit of a tart! Cranmer chickened out and sent the King a note. This was all going on as Henry was giving thanks in church for his perfect wife, and had congregations throughout the land giving thanks for Katherine's virtues. The letter concentrated on Katherine's relationship with Dereham, the one who had since come to work at Henry's court and started acting like a know-it-all. Cranmer was summoned to Henry's private chamber and told to launch an investigation. Katherine was confined to quarters for the duration of the investigation, to be released when her name had been cleared. It never was, and Henry never saw his Queen again. Tudor attitudes were that if Katherine had been easy with her morals before marriage, maybe she could be again, after marriage. It was a risk to the King's happiness and to the succession, which could not be taken. The telltales were all questioned again, and it came to Henry's attention that Katherine had employed Dereham as her private secretary. Even if she had given him a job to keep him sweet and keep him quiet, it did not look good. It made Henry look like an idiot. He was persuaded that she had either betrayed him or most certainly would. After a year of marriage, he had her beheaded on the grounds of adultery.

Two of her suspected lovers were arrested and Katherine questioned many times by Cranmer. He tried to extract a confession in return for compassion. One part of this scandal relates to whether or not there had been a marriage contract between Francis Dereham and Katherine. It was the equivalent to being engaged, but in Tudor times this was a legally binding contract. If Katherine had said 'yes', then her marriage to Henry VIII would have been illegal, null and void, and technically she could not have been tried for adultery. She may well have been kicked out, but with her head still attached to her shoulders. Katherine was too young and not experienced or bright enough to realise this strategy, although it had not worked for her cousin Anne Boleyn. There was nobody to advise her, all her family had distanced themselves from King and court, fearing for their own heads. Katherine was alone throughout.

There was also a rumour that she had agreed to marry Thomas Culpepper, who was now in the King's service. He too was arrested and questioned. Chambermaids and former associates were questioned, and stories of being with other men when she was about 13 or 14 were told. There was not any hard evidence throughout most of the investigation, and it seems as though Katherine may have been taken back by Henry. He had been keeping himself away so he would not cave in and feel sorry for her. Cranmer was like a dog with a bone trying to find evidence. He wanted to get rid of Katherine because they had such opposing religious views and he had started the entire investigation. Cranmer was indeed building up a case against Katherine, who was forced to make some sort of confession and mercy plea. Culpepper's name appeared again, with accusations of being alone with her for long periods of time, in many locations. Henry's heart was broken and his pride shattered. Alison Weir in *Six Wives of Henry VIII* says it is from this time forward that Henry became an old man. He had wanted to annul his marriage to Katherine. Execution was looking more likely by the day though. Katherine had allegedly laid almost naked with Dereham, written a love letter to Culpepper, which was her downfall, accused Dereham of raping her and embarrassed the King. To all intents and purpose she was being painted as a royal tart that had been round the block, and carried on when she was married to Henry. Despite the lack of evidence, this was the scandal that surrounded Katherine Howard. This was the scandal that was on the lips of the nation; by now it had become public knowledge and there were rumours he was going to take back Anne of Cleves. The Council was desperate to get a damning confession from anyone involved. They even tortured Dereham's friend by pulling out his teeth. A decision was made that there was enough evidence against Katherine, and she was executed on the 13th February 1542. She was laid to rest near Anne Boleyn at the Tower of London.

KATHERINE PARR
b.1512 d.1548 (also called Lady Latimer)
Married Henry VIII in 1543

The twice married (and widowed) Katherine Parr was of great comfort to Henry in his final years, with his painful ulcerous leg. He was even more cantankerous than usual by now, being in pain every day. Katherine almost got sent to the Tower, after being too vocal in her views about religious issues, and because she was not bearing sons. She outlived him, and managed to keep her head, after they had been together for three years.

SUMMARY

Catholics would argue that Henry's biggest scandal was the break from Rome, the destruction of Papal property, the confiscation of Papal lands and valuables, and the execution of those who opposed his idea for a Church of England, with the monarch as Supreme Governor. It was, of course, a big issue at the time, when religion was paramount in the lives of ordinary people. Breaking with Rome, showing disrespect to the Pope was a huge scandal, and cannot be underestimated. Meanwhile, Henry had become rather ruthless and tyrannical during his reign, executing many people, including two of his closest advisors; Thomas Cromwell and Sir Thomas More. His former chief minister Cardinal Wolsey had been summoned to the Tower of London but died on the way. He had started his reign as a young, vibrant, energetic king. He was popular with the people, but became a ruthless tyrant. In 1541 there was an uprising against the

King, in the north of England. Henry was quick to put it down, execute the ring leaders and forgive the locals. But these troubles were linked to what Alison Weir calls one of the worst atrocities of Henry's reign, which sickened even the Tudor court. It was linked to the grisly and bloody execution of Margaret Pole, Lady Salisbury. She was an old remnant of the Plantagenets, whom Henry VII had defeated. Henry VIII was nervous they might muster up support, and one day try and challenge his crown. The family's Catholicism was also seen as a major threat by Henry. Either as an overreaction, or to show his opponents his unrivalled power within the realm, he decided to have Lady Salisbury executed. She had served Henry VIII with loyalty and had never posed a threat to him in any way. She was in the tower because of her son's disloyalty.

She, however, had never showed any interest, vocal or otherwise, in returning to the old days of power for her family connections. She was also 68 years old, which was fairly ancient in those days. Henry was determined to carry out the execution. Lady Salisbury carved out a message on her cell wall, saying that only traitors should be sent to the block, and that she was certainly no traitor. All her protestations had fallen on deaf ears though. In the spring of 1541, Lady Salisbury was taken to the scaffold on Tower Green and publicly executed. The executioner was upset by his intended victim, maybe because of her age. We do not know for sure, but what we do know is that he somehow completely lost his nerve and skill all in one go, to the horror of even the blood thirsty crowd. Instead of one, clean, clear, sharp and quick slice through the neck, to deliver a humane killing, he got it badly wrong, missing several times. He ended up plunging his axe into her shoulder, through part of her head, the side of her neck until he had finally finished her off, like an amateur butcher. Reports claim that it took 11 blows to finish off the job. One hundred and fifty people looked on in horror. It was grisly, even by Tudor standards.

MARY BOLEYN
b.1503 d.1543

Best known for her suspected affair with King Henry VIII, and for being Anne Boleyn's sister. One could argue there is not really much of a scandal when it comes to kings, and for that matter queens, having a string of lovers and plenty of affairs. Indeed, within the pages of this book you can read about kings with many mistresses and even more 'bastard' children as they used to like to describe them. But one story within these realms deserves the title of 'scandalous' more than most, in my view. This is the tale of King Henry VIII and his affairs with Anne AND Mary Boleyn. That's right he had BOTH sisters.

Mary had two children and it is rumoured that both were Henry VIII's. Mary married Sir William Carey in 1520; she gave birth to a daughter and a son. Henry was even at her wedding. It is not known exactly when he decided to take Mary as his mistress, but it was before he fell for her sister Anne Boleyn. Nobody knows for sure who was the elder of the two girls, the conclusive evidence is simply not there. Henry was supposed to be good friends with Sir William Carey, despite sleeping with the man's wife. Josephine Wilkinson has written about Mary Boleyn in depth and points out one strong argument for Henry NOT being the father of Mary's children: that is he was known for his desire for being the only man in a woman's life. This brings into question the whole affair. Wilkinson points out that Henry got rid of Anne of Cleves, not just because she was not very good looking, but because he thought someone had been there before him! But she concludes that after weighing up 'all' the evidence, there are clues that both of Mary's children were from her affair with the King.

There is also plenty of circumstantial evidence to suggest Henry did father Mary's children or that he was at least sleeping with her. There is a story about a Member of Parliament insulting the King by suggesting he was sleeping with Anne's mother and sister. The King apparently replied that it was not true he was sleeping with the mother. Henry granted the Careys manors and estates during the affair and just before little Henry's birth. Before, the Careys had been granted rather minor offices, and that was all. These gifts may have been some kind of a sweetener, so Henry VIII could carry on having his sexual fun with the young Mary. Do not forget, King Henry also had another illegitimate son, also called Henry (FitzRoy), and as for Mary Boleyn's little son Henry, people would often comment about how he rather resembled the King in the looks department.

But there is even more drama to this story. Mary was rumoured to have been a mistress of King Francis I of France, Henry's rival. She apparently had several other affairs in France at the time as well, amongst the royal courtiers. It did not go unnoticed either. Many commented on her behaviour and she came home under a cloud of disgrace.

There is no proof of her affair with King Francis I, but many rumours. He used to refer to her as 'a great prostitute, more famous than them all'. But back to her affair with Henry VIII. He denied the rumours that he was father to one of Mary's children, because by now he was trying to woo her sister Anne, and wanted to pretend he had not been sleeping with the sister. Probably in this day and age, he would be called a rat! Anne had witnessed how Henry VIII had used Mary and cast her aside so easily. This is probably why she played so hard to get once Henry had set his sights on sister number two. The rumour that little baby Henry was the King's son appears to have been based on the recollection of John Hales, vicar of Isleworth, who 10 years after little Henry was born, told a monk from south London that a monk had once showed him 'young Master Carey' saying he was the King's bastard. It is not much historical evidence to go on though.

This could be described as the saucy scandal, Henry bedding one sister, getting her pregnant and chasing the other, and marrying her and getting her pregnant. But historically, the bigger scandal was arguably Mary's choice of second husband after she became a widow in 1528. First husband Sir William Carey died of the 'sweats'. Considering Mary was mixing in royal circles and was known at court, it would have been more conventional for her family to help choose a husband, to help her better herself. Instead, she married a man beneath her financially and socially. This was unusal in Tudor times. Her family were furious. In 1534, Mary secretly got married to a commoner, soldier William Stafford. It is fair to assume it was a match made from love.

The couple were banished from the royal court, and Mary's family stopped speaking to her. Her father cut off her allowance. They had expected something better from a woman who was by now, sister to the Queen of England. Henry had married Anne, and she later gave birth to the future Queen Elizabeth I.

Interestingly, Mary became broke and begged the King and her own relatives to help, but none of them would allow her into the family circle again. It was her sister Anne who sent her gold and money on the quiet. Two years later Anne was executed for treason. Being made an outcast from the family probably saved Mary's neck. When Anne was executed, many of her family fell out of favour with the King. She was at a safe distance out in Rochford, in Essex. When her parents died Mary inherited some property in Essex and spent the rest of her days with her second husband, until her death in 1543. She had two more children.

LADY JANE GREY
b. 1537 d. 1554
Reigned for just nine days in 1553, and nicknamed
'The Nine Days Queen'

After Henry VIII's only son, Edward VI, died as a child, there was a fight amongst the family over who would take the throne: a fight between Catholics and Protestants within the same family. It resulted in the execution of a child queen. Jane was beheaded at the age of just 16, after being Queen for a few days. Although she ascended to the throne, she did not get as far as a coronation. The history books always refer to her as Lady Jane Grey, rather than Queen Jane. Jane was Queen for just nine days in 1553, a de facto monarch. Some historians count her reign from the death of her predecessor; others from the actual proclamation. Therefore she's sometimes called the Thirteen Days Queen. Either way, she is the shortest serving monarch in English history. Sadly, she was just a family and political pawn to try and stop the Catholic Mary Tudor taking the throne.

Jane was the great-granddaughter of Henry VII, through her mother Lady Frances Brandon. She was a grandniece of Henry VIII. As 10-year-old girl she entered the household of Katherine Parr, Henry VIII's last queen, in about 1546. After being tutored by Protestants, she now experienced Protestant culture at court. She was a very well educated young girl, knowledgeable in the arts, as well as languages. Historical writer Alison Weir calls her one of the finest female minds of the century. Jane started to appear at court in 1551, after her father was made Duke of Suffolk, experiencing more Protestant views from the Duke of Northumberland, who was regent to the King Edward VI, who was too young to rule himself. In 1553 Jane married Northumberland's son Lord Guildford Dudley.

As the young King Edward was dying, the Duke of Northumberland persuaded him to declare his half-sisters Mary and Elizabeth as illegitimate, and alter the line of succession to Jane. The 15-year-old King Edward overruled the Third Succession Act before dying in July 1553. The Third Succession Act of 1543 had restored Elizabeth and Mary to the line of succession, despite the fact they were regarded as illegitimate. The Act also authorised Henry VIII to change the line of succession in his will. Henry had reinforced the succession of all three of his children. Mary's supporters therefore saw her as the rightful heir to the throne after Edward, followed by

Elizabeth. The fact that the dying King Edward changed Henry VIII's wishes was seen as weak and a challengeable claim to the throne by Lady Jane Grey.

Jane was proclaimed queen within days. She was arguably the first proper English queen regnant. But Mary Tudor had been plotting, and had been holed up in Suffolk with her supporters, now growing in number. Support for Jane dwindled, even from her own family. Mary marched into London and was crowned with Parliament's full support. Jane and her husband Lord Guilford Dudley were both charged with high treason, together with two of Dudley's brothers. Their trial, by a special commission, took place on 13 November 1553, at the Guildhall in the City of London. Jane, her husband and her father were beheaded.

MARY QUEEN OF SCOTS
Tragic Heroine or Conniving Murderer?
b. 1542 d.1587 (executed)

There was so much scandal surrounding Mary Queen of Scots, she could almost certainly be renamed Mary Queen of Scandal. I have left out her dates of reign because of her complicated accession, forced abdication and her marriage into a foreign royal family. She was executed by her cousin Elizabeth I after been held prisoner in England for nearly 19 years. She had a difficult life, and was followed by controversies and problems. Mary was the daughter of King James V of Scotland. She became Queen of Scotland at just six days old following the death of her father. Her mother, Mary of Guise, sent Mary to France to escape the factions plotting to gain control of her on Scottish soil. The Scottish Lords were taking advantage of her and refused to accept her authority because she was just a little girl. Mary was sent away to France, where she married Francis, later Francis II. This was arguably the best time of her life. She mixed with the royal family, was well liked and lived a life of luxury between royal residences. But she had a run of bad luck, all before she was 18. Her father-in-law was killed in 1559 in a jousting accident, her husband died in 1560 as a 16-year-old, and Mary also lost her mother who was still in Scotland.

Mary decided to go back to Scotland in 1561, at the age of 18. She landed at Leith on 19 August. In 1565 she married her cousin Lord Darnley, a dashing 22-year-old man. However, he was widely hated in Scotland, with a reputation as a bad-tempered drunk.

Her troubles began and the scandals occurred soon after Mary arrived back in Scotland. Mary's problem was her tolerance to others. She was a Catholic, but recognised Protestant reforms. Both sides disrespected her for sitting on the fence. So she displeased everyone, whilst trying to please everybody. After she married Henry Stewart, Lord Darnley in 1565, her half-brother James Stuart, the Earl of Moray, raised a rebellion of nobles against her, but was defeated. When her marriage to Darnley was on the rocks, a group of Protestant lords murdered Mary's personal secretary, the Italian man David Rizzio, in front of her. Darnley had decided Mary and David had been spending a little bit too much time together. A year later, Mary had given birth to the future King James I of England, and had formed a close and special relationship with James Hepburn, the Earl of Bothwell, after enduring a stressful marriage to Darnley.

By now, it was clear that Bothwell was Mary's favourite. The first scandal arose when Mary left Darnley at home to ride off somewhere, only for the house to be blown up. Darnley was later found in the garden, strangled. Somebody had finished off the job that the explosion had failed to do; soon after Bothwell and Mary got married. Bothwell stood trial, being the chief suspect, but it was a very quick trial and he was cleared. This suspicious sequence of events didn't do much for Mary's reputation and some of her closest supporters were very quick to desert her. The nobles all gathered their forces and faced up to Mary and Bothwell, challenging them head on. Bothwell fled abroad and was never seen again, and Mary was captured and put behind bars at Lochleven Castle. Here, she was forced to give up her throne in favour of her young son James. She did manage to escape though, and raise an army but was defeated at the battle of Langslide in 1568. It's at this point she fled to England with the plan of getting Elizabeth I to back her claim to regain the Scottish throne. Mary was seized at the border and imprisoned by the English. She was confident that Elizabeth would help her, queen to queen, and as family. But she was wrong. In some ways Mary was a threat to Elizabeth I. The root of the problem, as so often in these times, was religion. Elizabeth I was a Protestant but tolerated quiet Catholics who worshipped without making a fuss. This was the opposite of her predecessor, and half-sister, Mary I who liked to kill non-Catholics. It is possible that Elizabeth saw Mary Queen of Scots as being a potential leader or figure head for the Catholics in England. The other scandal, as far as some were concerned, was the fact that Elizabeth I was considered illegitimate, and therefore an imposter on the throne. Conveniently, Mary Queen of Scots was the nearest legal, genealogical heir. This was based on the view by some people at the time that Henry VIII (Elizabeth's father), married Anne Boleyn (Elizabeth's mother), without a recognised divorce or annulment of Henry's marriage to Catherine of Aragon.

The second scandal is the claim that Mary was behind numerous plots to overthrow the Protestant Queen Elizabeth I. The most serious scheme was the Babington plot, which directly called for the assassination of Elizabeth. By now, Elizabeth was faced with a dilemma; keep Mary alive and free in England and risk a Catholic uprising against her own throne, or send her cousin and a legal monarch back to a country where she would have almost certainly been killed. Elizabeth kept her guarded in various houses and castles for 19 years, and never met her. Eventually Mary was put on trial and beheaded in 1587. Elizabeth was against executing an anointed queen. She signed the death warrant to keep her nobles happy, but demanded it be kept locked away. However, the warrant was taken straight to the jail and Mary was executed before Elizabeth even realised.

So far, the scandal has centred on the 'mysterious' death of her second husband Darnley and her sudden marriage to number three. But there's another side to this scandal. Mary had some letters tucked away inside a casket. They included marriage contracts, sonnets, poems and letters. Mary's enemies claimed the contents of the casket letters were detailed proof of both Mary's and Bothwell's plans to murder Darnley. In *Mary Queen of Scots and the Casket Letters* A.E. MacRoberts says if the letters are genuine, they give real evidence against Mary and the excuse Elizabeth I needed to have detained her for so long. But would Mary have been so stupid to have written down such incriminating evidence. The events of 1567–8 ruined her reputation across the whole of Europe. She may well have been an innocent bystander. Perhaps she didn't have anything to do with the death of her second husband, whether or not number three killed him. But how scandalous that a Scottish queen be incarcerated for nearly two decades and then executed on the evidence of these easily forgeable casket letters. We can't make up our own minds with any certainty, because the originals disappeared a long time ago, back in 1584. All we have are the translations and copies made in 1568. It has generated four-hundred years of debate among historians. Did Mary's enemies forge or plant the letters to get the evidence needed to secure a conviction against her and the execution of an innocent queen, or was she a scheming, lying, ambitious, murdering adulteress who deserved everything she got?

KEY DATES FOR MARY, QUEEN OF SCOTS
b.1542 d.1587
Father: James V; Mother: Mary of Guise
Made Queen at six days old and crowned nine months later.

1543	Treaties of Greenwich promised a marriage between Mary and Edward, with any heirs to get a united kingdom
1544–51	Henry VIII started raids on Scotland to bully them into Mary Queen of Scots marriage. Mary moved around and hid in castles
1547	Mary of Guise asked for French help against English, they asked for Mary Queen of Scots to be sent over for marriage
1548–61	Raised in French Court
1558	Married Francis, Dauphine of France, later Francis II
1559	Mary becomes Queen Consort of France
1560	Mary widowed
1561	Returned to Scotland
1565	She married Henry Stuart, Lord Darnley (her cousin) descendant of Margaret Tudor – unhappy marriage
1566	Their son James born
1567	A plot hatched to remove Darnley, explosion at house in Kirk O'Field, found dead in garden
1567	April – Mary abducted on her way to Edinburgh – taken to Dunbar Castle and allegedly raped
1567	A month later returned to Edinburgh, married Bothwell.
1567	Scots nobility turned against them, army faced Mary and Bothwell
1567	Two months later Lords took Mary to Lochleven Castle, imprisoned her, she miscarried twins and was forced to abdicate in favour of her baby son James
1568	Mary escaped, raised an army, was defeated and fled to England
1568	Imprisoned by Elizabeth's Officer at Carlisle, then Bolton Castle, then Tutbury Castle
1568/9	Elizabeth I ordered inquiry into Darnley murder. Mary

refused to acknowledge authority of the hearing, as she was an anointed queen, James Stewart now ruling Scotland and running the inquiry. He wanted Mary and supporters kept out of Scotland. Inquiry based on eight caskets

1570   Charles IX of France asked Elizabeth I to help Mary regain her throne

1586   Mary implicated in Babington plot, sanctioning attempted assassination of Elizabeth I

1587   Mary Queen of Scots was executed on English soil, after her trial

THE SCANDAL OF THE BURIED PALACE

A Surrey housing estate now sits on top of one of the most fascinating Tudor palaces in England, Oatlands Palace. We can't get hold of some of that history, because new homes have been built on top of it. Some archaeology has been completed around the homes. So how did one of Henry VIII's homes almost become forgotten?

Oatlands Palace started out as Oatlands Manor, a Sixteenth Century house owned by the Reade family. By the mid–1530s Henry VIII had taken ownership of the property and moved into the building. Repairs began in 1537, followed by a major building project to turn the manor into a palace fit for a king. Henry liked Oatlands because it was near Hampton Court and Nonsuch Palace, where he liked to hunt. The plan for Oatlands was for it to be a home for his new Queen, Anne of Cleves. However, when he realised how ugly she was, that plan was aborted.

Oatlands is steeped in Tudor history. It is here that Henry married Catherine Howard, on the 28 July 1540. Elizabeth I stayed at the palace to escape the plague in London, and other royals have lived there, including Anne of Denmark and Henrietta Maria (wives of James I and Charles I respectively). After King Charles I was beheaded in 1649, Cromwell destroyed much of the estate, stripping it bare, before selling off what was left. When Charles II returned to the throne in 1660 Oatlands, now just a small manor and vineyard, became Crown property again and was leased to various noblemen through the 1600s and 1700s. The Seventh Earl of Lincoln built Oatlands House there in the 1720s, five-hundred metres east of the original palace site. Further buildings and gardens were added. In 1789 the Duke and Duchess of York moved into Oatlands House. In 1822 the estate was divided up and part of the land sold off. The

Archaeological digs at Oatlands, around the houses, in the late 1960s. Printed by kind permission of Elmbridge Museum, Elmbridge Borough Council c. Excavations continued until 1970. Further excavations were carried out 1983–4 when part of the Palace site was being redeveloped. Digs were obviously restricted to areas which had not yet been built on.

House became a hotel in 1856 and the lands became a commercial market garden. In 1919 the market gardens were bought by Weybridge Urban District Council and developed as a housing estate. This process was repeated on other parts of the estate in 1950. Today, only a few walls and a gate have survived the days of a once great royal palace and gardens. Archaeological digs have taken place at the site over the years. The first major dig started in 1968, over three-hundred years after Oatlands was destroyed. The project was determined to establish more about the palace's position and construction. Digging today is limited, as there is a major housing estate right on top of it.

QUEEN ELIZABETH I – THE GOLDEN AGE
b. 1533 d. 1603
Reigned: 1558 –1603

Queen Elizabeth I reigned over England in what become known as the Golden Age or Elizabethan era, a fascinating period in royal history. She ruled during the defeat of the Spanish Armada, Sir Walter Raleigh's adventures, Shakespeare's plays and at a time of discovery in the world of the arts and literature. She is best known for not getting married and her 'is she, isn't she?' relationship with Lord Robert Dudley.

She claimed the throne on the basis of the Third Succession Act of 1543, which put her next in line, after Edward VI and Mary I. It had been a turbulent time. Henry VIII had died in 1547 leaving his son Edward VI as a child king. Edward died as a teenager. Lady Jane Grey ruled for nine days, before Edward's half-sister Mary I snatched back the throne; she died childless in 1558, in her early forties. Her half-sister Elizabeth then took over. Immediately after her accession, Parliament called for Elizabeth to name a successor. She was nervous about doing this as a successor could try and usurp her. Mary Queen of Scots was a possible contender but was not a popular choice because she was with the hated King of France, and she was a Catholic. In addition, Henry VIII's last will and testament had banned the Stuarts from the line of succession. Parliament petitioned Elizabeth to marry and name an heir but she did not want to be ordered about and pressurised by Parliament. Options were running out, as was Elizabeth's biological clock. By 1567 Mary Queen of Scots was no longer a possibility as a successor after the scandal surrounding the murder of her own husband Lord Darnley. Other contenders were

Queen Elizabeth I 'I may not be a lion, but I am a lion's cub, and I have a lion's heart'

either Catholic or beneath Elizabeth. It left the Earl of Huntingdon and the alien James VI of Scotland as the nearest contenders.

It can be argued that Elizabeth's seemingly lack of interest or action about marrying, producing an heir and a stable monarchy and country, was a continuing scandal of the Elizabethan era. It was a serious matter, but she played one suitor off against another, keeping everyone guessing. It was her teasing 'wait and see' manner that captivated her subjects and worried her advisors. She kept people wondering for decades. At the start of her reign European ambassadors were racing to promote their masters as possible husbands for the new Queen of England. Marriage offers came from many royal houses across Europe. The website *elizabethi.org* describes Elizabeth I as the most sought after woman in Europe and the only person who did not seem to understand the urgency for marriage.

Elizabeth herself said, 'If I followed the inclination of my nature, it is this, beggar woman and single, far rather than Queen and married.' She described herself as being bound to a husband called England. Elizabeth seemed to have had little regard for the continuation of the Tudor dynasty, otherwise marriage and children would have been an urgent priority. It was in complete contrast to her father King Henry VIII who was obsessed with the matter of succession, marrying six times to try and have sons. Elizabeth saw her love-life as a personal matter and even told Parliament to stop demanding an announcement from her on the matter.

It can be argued that Elizabeth was putting off marriage through fear of ending up with a Catholic husband. At the time, a suitor's religion was just as important as his nationality and social standing. She was no doubt fearful of potential uprisings between Catholics and Protestants as a result of a mixed marriage. Susan Doran points out in *Monarchy and Matrimony: The Courtships of Elizabeth I*, that Elizabeth's husband would be joint Supreme Governor of the Church of England, making it difficult to practice a religion different from the one established by law. Therefore, perhaps one of the reasons Elizabeth was not rushing to pick one of her suitors, was the number of 'Catholic' men being offered, which she saw as undermining the stability of the country. In addition, the Old Testament warns about mixed marriages: Deuteronomy 7, against a union between Canaanites and Israelites, and Exodus 34 against Israelites and idolaters, in the Mosaic Law. People lived by religion and the Bible back then. Most would have known about this warning and taken it very seriously.

Did Elizabeth intend to remain unmarried or did political, religious and historical events shape the outcome? She certainly had a selection of suitors, some more eligible than others. She made no secret though of her continued desire to stay single. In 1566, Elizabeth responded to a Parliamentary delegation about their concerns over her marriage and the succession. She plainly told them she would marry when she was ready, and not before. As for succession, she said it was a serious matter for her consideration but did not give much away in her reply. She likened Parliament trying to organise her life, as a foot telling the head what to do instead of the other way round. Elizabeth's demands became too high for foreign suitors, with agreements about their religion and being subservient to her, unappealing to many. Christopher Haigh's *Elizabeth I* referred to her as 'a royal tease rather than a royal tart'. Elizabeth's early years were fraught with scandal and upset. Her mother (Anne Boleyn) was executed by her father (Henry VIII), two of her step-mothers had died, and her sister's mother (Catherine of Aragon) had been cut off from husband Henry VIII for not bearing sons, having her marriage annulled. A young impressionable Elizabeth would almost certainly have been affected by these events, and it would have created an impression on her about what happens to women who get married. Some historians have indeed argued in favour of the theory that Elizabeth was put off sexual relations and the idea of marriage after seeing her father Henry VIII going through six marriages, and her mother being executed. However, this is using modern day thinking to solve Sixteenth-Century living. Monarchs were there to rule and punish and there were fatal consequences if you were found guilty of treason or other serious crimes.

THE SCANDALS

As if it wasn't enough of a scandal to avoid marriage and deny England an heir to the throne, and a guarantee of the continuation of the royal dynasty, there were other scandals. Indeed her lack of marital and breeding actions resulted in the ending of the Tudor line in 1603. In Elizabethan times, the fact that she seemed carefree about creating or even naming an heir, thus jeopardising England's peace and security, was in itself scandalous. With no heir and an uncertain future, England may have been vulnerable to civil war or a target for foreign invasion. On top of this underlying and continuing serious problem, there were also a number of scandalous incidents and events that are well documented.

THE YOUNG PRINCESS ELIZABETH AND A NEW FATHER FIGURE

Turning back the clock to when Elizabeth was just a young teenager, she had quite a difficult time. The Queen Dowager Katherine Parr, married Thomas Seymour, brother of the Lord Protector Edward Seymour, just after Henry VIII's death. Elizabeth was packed off to live with Katherine and her new husband. However, things did not quite go smoothly, as Thomas took an unhealthy shine to the young pretty Elizabeth. It has been suggested that she also had a crush on him, and that he took advantage of it, as he was in his late thirties by now. The story goes that he often visited her in her bedchamber first thing in the morning. Unusually though, some reports suggest Katherine went too. Some historians have written about this incident in the context of Elizabeth being sexually abused by an older man. They claim this put her off sex and marriage later in life. Others, however, have called this complete rubbish and say there is a lack of proof about what happened. We only know a part of this story from information that came out of an inquiry into the incident later on. But if you think this is far-fetched, there are conspiracy theories about Elizabeth getting pregnant in later years and having a child on the quiet. This would have been the biggest scandal of them all, had it been true. It would have finished off the monarchy, perhaps for good. But this conspiracy is ridiculous. Meanwhile, we do not know exactly what really went on between Thomas and Elizabeth, and never will. Perhaps it was horse-play, misunderstood, exaggerated, or maybe it was child molestation. However, it seems as though things did get out of control between the two of them, and came to a head when Katherine found them alone too many times and got jealous of all the attention her husband was paying the young girl. Katherine thought the best course of action was for Elizabeth to leave the marital household. Katherine died in childbirth soon after and Thomas unsuccessfully sought Elizabeth's hand in marriage.

PLAN TO KIDNAP EDWARD

When Henry VIII died in 1547, his son became King Edward VI, at the tender age of nine. The boy's uncle, Edward Seymour, became Protector of England, effectively ruling on his behalf. Henry had reinstated his daughters in the line of succession. This meant they could be used as political pawns. After Edward VI, Mary was next in line to the throne, then Elizabeth. But a scandal was brewing because the Protector's younger brother, Thomas Seymour, as mentioned above, was jealous of Edward's power and tried to overthrow him. He tried to kidnap little Edward, a plan that cost Thomas his life. But Thomas had declared his longing to marry Elizabeth. She was therefore implicated in this treasonous plot. As a teenage princess, she had to do battle with her interrogators, argue her case and prove her innocence.

ELIZABETH'S SECRET LOVER

As Queen, did Elizabeth really have a secret lover? If she did it was the worst kept secret ever. Some say Lord Robert Dudley, later the Earl of Leicester, was her lover. Others argue they were just very close friends. Some suggest it was merely flirtatious courtly love, as was common in the day. Elizabeth herself referred to him as a brother, but they were always sniggering together in dark corners like young lovers. And anyone knew if they wanted to get to see the Queen or wanted her to agree to something, they had to get to Dudley first, during his years of favour at least. Of course nobody can be absolutely sure whether or not Elizabeth was having sex with her favourite courtier. In *Monarchy and Matrimony* Susan Doran says an unexpected pregnancy would have rocked the monarchy and Elizabeth was far too politically astute to risk that. Elizabeth had to entertain the idea of marrying a foreign dignitary because marriage back then was used as a diplomatic bargaining tool, to secure allies abroad and the crown at home. Marrying Dudley would have brought none of these advantages. But more importantly Dudley was already married to someone else. Was Elizabeth having an affair with a married courtier?

It was accepted for kings to have many mistresses, but for a queen regnant absolutely not. There were certainly whisperings at court and questions being raised about Elizabeth's relationship and intentions when it came to the married Dudley. There is absolutely no known proof of really went on between Elizabeth and Dudley. Their friendship certainly was scandalous at times, mainly because of his marriage. But Susan Doran is probably right, and Elizabeth could not afford the risks of having an illegitimate baby. Nobody knew then, or knows now, the true nature of their relationship, although she had talked of their relationship as that of a brother and sister. There was certainly plenty of talk at court about their relationship. Dudley became synonymous with the label 'possible lover' and 'maybe future husband' for Elizabeth. Historians have argued, did they or didn't they, were they an item or weren't they. It can be argued the rumours about the romance between Dudley and Elizabeth stopped her getting married to anyone else, or perhaps she really did not want to marry anyone but him, thus in the long term, affecting the line of succession.

In Agnes Strickland's *The Life of Queen Elizabeth I* she says, their 'special relationship' was the talk of the court. Of course, royal courts had spies who reported to their masters overseas. It is not unreasonable to suggest news of Elizabeth's closeness to Dudley, no matter how innocent or not, may have reached foreign royal courts and put off some potential suitors. Elizabeth was leaving England open to chaos at best, invasion or civil war at worst, if she had died without an heir. It can be argued it was scandalous behaviour not to marry and have children, but also dangle promises and the mysterious lady routine in front of her councillors who genuinely cared about the succession and the future of the realm. William Cecil, the Queen's Chief Minister, summed up his concerns:

> 'And then shall she leave her crown in question, the religion in debate, her people divided for both, and her realm answerable for infinite injuries to all nations'

But there was a bigger problem. Dudley's wife Amy Robsart was very ill. Was he (and the Queen) waiting for Amy to pass away before going public with their relationship? That's guess work and we'll never know, because Amy was found dead at the bottom of the stairs in her house. Gossip at the time asked 'was she pushed?' There was no way Elizabeth could marry Robert now. It certainly looked like they had finished off his wife so they could be together. If Elizabeth had married Dudley after his wife was found dead, it would have ruined her reputation, and she knew that. It was a serious scandal back then, but medical knowledge now suggests Amy may have had brittle bones, explaining why her legs gave way. Recent suggestions therefore show Amy may well have died as a result of a medical condition rather than being pushed down the stairs by someone. This was far too medically advanced for someone to have understood at the time. Breast cancer can also soften the bones and a simple trip may have had fatal consequences. We do know that Amy had a 'malady of the breast'. In *Elizabeth I* Rosalind K. Marshall points out that many people in England and France thought Amy had been murdered, and Dudley was responsible. Ambassadors and advisors warned Elizabeth against marrying him. Amy's maid did not help when she ruled out the possibility of suicide, by declaring her mistress was far too religious to contemplate taking her own life.

To make the scandal even worse, Dudley did not even attend Amy's inquest and funeral. In short, a queen getting her married lover's wife bumped off so they can be together? That was the scandal and that was the gossip of the day throughout England and the rest of Europe. It is another part of history we will never know the actual truth about. But there is certainly no evidence to suggest a murderous plot was part of a major love plan. It certainly did not look good though. The gossip was very damaging to Elizabeth, but things would have been much worse if she had married Dudley after the event. In 1578 Dudley married someone else, Lettice Devereux, Countess of Essex, the Queen's cousin. He did fall out of favour with Elizabeth, but she always cherished their good times together. He wrote to her just before he died in 1588, probably from an infection, and Elizabeth marked it 'his last letter'. It was found in her treasure box when she passed away, 15 years later. His tomb can be seen at St Mary's Church in Warwickshire. During his time Dudley was a powerful and influential figure, holding a number of privileged titles and carrying out royal duties, because of his close relationship with Queen Elizabeth I. They included Master of the Queen's Horse, Constable of Windsor Castle, Commander of the English forces in the Netherlands and Privy Council member.

AND FINALLY – A LITTLE TOUCHY AREN'T WE?

In 1579 John Stubbs wrote a pamphlet called *The Discoverie of a Gaping Gulf* (sic). In it he made a serious attack against the proposed marriage of Elizabeth and one of her suitors, the Duke of Anjou, saying England would be swallowed up by another French marriage. Elizabeth was furious there was 'opinion' on her proposed marriage. She ordered that his right hand be chopped off, in public, at the wrist with a butcher's cleaver. Stubbs took his punishment like a man and with his left hand raised his hat and shouted 'God Save the Queen', then fainted. William Page, the publisher, had the same punishment. The printer was pardoned. Lots of the pamphlets were burned and destroyed. In 1603 Elizabeth I died. Her councillors had been taking part in secret negotiations with King James VI of Scotland to take up the crown in a smooth and peaceful transition. He later became King James I of England. From this point in history England and Scotland have shared a sovereign, except for the interregnum.

MARY I (BLOODY MARY)
b. 1516 d.1558
Reigned: 1553–1558

Mary was the daughter of Henry VIII and Catherine of Aragon. She had strong Catholic views and cruelly forced them onto the people of England. Henry of course destroyed much of Catholicism in England during his reign. When his son Edward VI took over in 1547, he too was a Protestant. When Mary eventually took to the throne, it was her chance to ruthlessly enforce her religion onto the country. And ruthless she was. Records are incomplete and not always a hundred per cent accurate, but from what we can establish, she burnt almost three hundred people at the stake for not being true and loyal Catholics. These became known as the Marian Persecutions and were her way of restoring the Catholic faith in the country. But she behaved no better than her father Henry VIII when it came to killing opponents. She was cruel and blood thirsty, and it has earned her the nickname, Bloody Mary. That's where the name of the drink comes from as well, the tomato juice in it representing the spilled blood of Mary's helpless victims. The persecutions lasted almost four years and dominated the history of Mary I. These executions and mass spilling of blood is what she is now remembered for.

Documents show there was no discrimination when it came to the choice of Mary's poor victims. They included: bishops, labourers, children, husbands, disabled people, labourers and virgins. Most were burnt at the stake; others were whipped, starved and imprisoned. Her cruelty knew no boundaries or limitations. Her actions generated a fear of Catholic extremism in England, feelings which also drove King

James II from the throne many years later. Laws were eventually passed to make sure no other Catholic ever again became monarch, and no reigning monarch ever married a Catholic; these were the Bill of Rights 1689 and the Act of Succession 1701. Mary's Catholic restoration was short lived. The two previous monarchs, Henry VIII and Edward VI (ignoring Lady Jane Grey for the moment), had pushed through anti-Catholic reforms during their reigns. Mary reversed them back to Catholicism. After Mary's death Protestantism became more accepted, as Elizabeth I was more tolerant. Mary's extremism and change of policy from the monarchy caused mayhem. One minute you were supposed to be a Catholic, the next there was a break with the Pope and the destruction of monasteries, then it was punishment by death for not being a Catholic, and then it was tolerance when Elizabeth I came to power. It was a turbulent and confusing time for many normal people. For those in politics, in the Privy Council, the advisors to the monarch, it became a career nightmare, because nobody knew which side they should take and how long it would last. Mary's conversion of England was hampered by the fact that the well off, who had bought cheap lands sold off by Henry VIII during the Dissolution of the Monasteries, had refused to hand the lands back to the Church. In 1555, Parliament repealed the anti-papal laws passed by Henry VIII and restored the ecclesiastical courts: but confiscated church property was not always given back.

There was relief and celebration when Mary died in 1558. Everyone was glad to see the back of her. Even her husband didn't like her that much. She was betrothed to the Holy Roman Emperor Charles V. This was arranged when she was just a child. These 'arranged' engagements were commonplace in these times, especially for royalty. Mary's proposed marriage, like many others, was for political reasons. There was nothing unusual about that at all. However, when she became Queen, she decided it would be more appropriate if she married the Emperor's son, Prince Philip, later Philip II of Spain. Parliament begged her to consider marrying an Englishman instead. They were worried that England would become a dependency of Spain, and Philip would have the real control in England. They were probably scared that as a woman Mary would not have been strong enough to keep control. She was, after all, 'just a woman'.

However Mary turned out to be a strong and formidable force. Unfortunately for Mary the English people were against her marriage, because they hated foreigners, and Mary had failed to win over any hearts and minds. They wed at Winchester Cathedral. The chair she sat in for the ceremony (a gift from the Pope), is still there for people to see to this day. After the wedding, there did not seem to be much affection between Mary and Philip. He seemed more interested in the fine figures of Mary's ladies-in-waiting than his own wife's vital statistics! Her marriage to Philip was childless; Philip spent most of it on the continent, he did not hang around England for long.

Mary thought she was pregnant a number of times, but probably had at least one phantom pregnancy. Health problems had in fact given her a swollen stomach. She never did have any children and died at the age of 42 at St. James's Palace, in 1558, and was interred at Westminster Abbey. Her half sister Elizabeth became Queen, and the last of the ruling Tudors. Mary's blood thirsty ways have earned her a place in the history books, for all the wrong reasons. She seems not to have known the meaning of the words tolerance or mercy.

IBRAHIM I OF TURKEY
b.1616 d.1648
Reigned 1640–1648

Ibrahim was called 'The Mad' and 'The Crazy One' and the story of his scandalous sexual cruelty towards women has been handed down through the years. He had been locked up for years before being proclaimed Sultan. He decided to make up for lost time by having his own non-stop sexual party. The previous Sultans had executed all their brothers except Ibrahim, although his death had been ordered as Murad IV took his final breath. But Ibrahim's mother stepped in to save him.

At the age of 23, Ibrahim decided he was going to start making up for all the time he had lost since being shut away. He had a thing for virgins and fat women. He had his agents go out and look for the fattest women they could find. They brought back a woman weighing nearly 23 stones and he was delighted with his 'catch'. Weirdly his mother was put in charge of organising an endless supply of virgins for her young son to break in. From time to time he would get a group of virgins assembled in his garden. He would order them to strip completely naked and he would ravage the ones he liked the look of, as they kicked and struggled to try and escape. Despite stories of his sexual antics, he was sometimes impotent, and his mother tried to help him with that as well. She gave him a number of aphrodisiacs to give him the urge. By now he had a harem of 280 women, all there to satisfy him on demand. He liked to get his girls to kick and scream and object to his advances, it was all part of his sexual kicks. But he did rape at least one woman, quite viciously, a women who rejected his marriage proposal upon her father's orders. He ravaged her for a few days, had his wicked way with her then sent her packing back to her father. By now a number of concubines in his palace were getting pregnant and there were a few babies around!

One day a rumour reached Ibrahim that one of his concubines had been 'contaminated' by an outsider. He went absolutely berserk! He did not know which of the girls had been taken advantage of. So he decided to get rid of them all and have a fresh start. But he did not fire them, pension them off, banish them from the palace or anything nearly as humane as that. He decided they all had to die. He had some of them tortured first. Then each girl was tied up in a sack, weighted down, and thrown into the sea. Only one of them survived. Eventually, after years of excess and corruption in the kingdom, Ibrahim was overthrown in a coup, imprisoned and executed by two guards, by strangulation. He had brought his country to a near state of collapse in just a few years.

THE HOUSE OF HABSBURG AND THEIR GENE PROBLEMS

The Habsburg dynasty was one of the most important and influential royal families in Europe dating back hundreds of years, generating rulers across the continent from Austria and Belgium, to the Netherlands, Spain, Hungary, and other places. The Habsburgs dominated European royalty as emperors, consorts and monarchs. Originally from Switzerland, they ruled Austria for hundreds of years, the Spanish Empire and territories by diplomatic marriage. In the 1500s, the senior Spanish and junior Austrian branches of the family went their separate ways. In 1700 its Spanish branch died out with the death of Spain's King Charles II, a sickly man, apparently impotent and infertile as well, which is never a great quality for a king.

It was the Habsburg's inbreeding that became a real scandal. *The Independent* newspaper's feature on the Habsburgs was called 'Revealed: the inbreeding that ruined the Habsburgs' and claimed the dynasty was undone by incest. They constantly bred amongst themselves, rarely allowing 'common' blood into the line. Cousins married each other, and uncles and nieces married and bred. Nine out of eleven marriages over two hundred years were between first cousins, or uncles and nieces. More distant family members added to the wonky gene pool. This policy had serious biological implications. Scientists who have studied the genealogy say the shallow end of the gene pool where Charles was created, was the same as if the child came from close incestuous sex.

The Habsburgs suffered many physical deformities in varying levels of seriousness. They included: late development of speech, premature ageing, hallucinations, swellings, weakness, rickets, bulbous lips and bigger than average sized heads, and sexual problems such as premature ejaculation. But there were also mental implications. According to the education website *msu.edu*, Charles II was actually retarded. Some reports suggest Charles of Spain had real trouble concentrating and taking things in. The most famous result of the incestuous inbreeding was the Habsburg lip, a disfiguringly prominent lower jaw, where the lower part grows faster than the top law (mandibular prognathism). Charles of Spain had a very serious version of this, as well as a huge tongue. He could not eat properly because of his jaw deformity. Dentists even today, refer to this deformity as the Habsburg jaw.

Foxnews.com published a piece on this and pointed out that the Habsburg's high infant and child mortality rates were another result of their inbreeding. It claimed only 50 per cent of their children made it to the age of 10, compared with 80 per cent amongst the commoners. Michael Farquhar's *A Treasury of Royal Scandals* calls them a 'genetic freak show from relentless inbreeding'.

WILLIAM III & MARY II – A CHANGE IN DIRECTION

WILLIAM III

b.1650 d.1702
Reigned 1689–1702

MARY II

b. 1662 d.1694
Reigned 1689–1694

- Is it a scandal that a Catholic cannot take the throne of this country?
- Is it a scandal that those in the line of succession would lose his or her place, if he or she even married a one?

- Would such discrimination be allowed today in other areas of work and religion? Probably not!
- Who and what is responsible for this decision, and how did this situation develop?

For this we should turn back the clock to the reign of King James II of England (also known as James VII of Scotland), and his successor, King William III and his wife Mary II. The years covering the reign of William III, witnessed profound changes in the relationship between monarchy and Parliament. This was the time of The Glorious Revolution. The nature of the monarchy itself underwent a number of developments during this time, with far reaching consequences. William himself, against a backdrop of religion, absolutism, finance and wars, contributed to the constitutional shift between 1688 and 1702. William III, who was a Dutch stadtholder (ruler) became King of England, Ireland and Scotland, jointly with his wife, as Queen Mary II. This was unusual in British history when a king and queen ruled as joint monarchs, with equal power. Mary was not a queen consort. William was only partly responsible for the changes though. James II started events partly by the way he ruled, which was unpopular with some. Parliament's growing authority also contributed to events. William's style of kingship completes the picture. The debate over finance for war, a standing army and the validity of the divine right of kings played a key part in all this as well. The nature of the monarchy changed because of the combination of these issues. It all led to Catholics being barred from the line of succession. It was the fact that James II of England lost his crown in the first place that started the chain of events between 1688 and 1702, under his replacement William. A study of James's nature of ruling, as a prelude and comparative to William is an important way to look at the bigger picture. Three issues in particular were at the centre of James's turbulent reign; his use of dispensing powers to further Catholic positions, his staunch belief in the divine right of kings, and the birth of his son. James tried to reverse laws that excluded Catholic from office. Using dispensing powers he could exempt Catholics from certain legislation. It led to a rise in the number of Catholic councillors, aristocrats, lecturers and army officers. In 1687, he issued the first Declaration of Indulgence to get former anti-popery Whigs to support him. With exiled Whigs plotting from abroad, Craig Rose, in *England in the 1690s Revolution, Religion and War* said it brought about a rare degree of Protestant unity. This sowed the seeds for William's intervention. James was packing Parliament with his own supporters. He wanted to repeal the Test Act and started to purge those in high office, under the crown, opposed to his ideas. He also created a standing army and replaced much of it with Catholics. James's opponents saw these steps as paving the way for arbitrary rule. Tim Harris in *Revolution* argues that James's regime collapsed from within due to widespread opposition to his policies to help co-religionists. He says there would have been some kind of revolution in 1688, with or without William. The situation was made worse when James fathered a son. Until then, opponents knew the throne would pass to his Protestant daughter, Mary. In addition, there was a clash between the ancient belief of the divine right of kings and the rights of Parliament. The ideology of a monarch's divine right, championed by royal houses such as the Stuarts and the House of Bourbon was starting to be questioned. This polemic attitude to the monarchy would later

William III & Mary II

help shape William's reign. Whigs and some Tories, were fearful of James's close friendship with Louis XIV (of France) and the prospect of a popish English state. They planned to resolve the crisis by inviting Europe's Dutch Protestant champion, William of Orange, to 'invade' England. James made concessions when he sensed a possible invasion. For example, he restored old city charters and abolished the Court of High Commission. Harris says James's actions, along with the birth of the prince, united Anglican and non-conformists against him. With the end of James II, came the end of the idea of divine right, whereby monarchs are given their position by God. English noblemen had been plotting for William of Orange to come over and save their liberties. William landed with his forces, and James witnessed enough desertions to William's side, to cause him to give up, eventually fleeing to France.

Tim Harris says James fled in the face of disaffection, rather than being beaten by an army. Several noblemen and bishops set up a provisional government and William recognised a power vacuum, realising he could accept the Crown. He called together the Convention Parliament, which offered him the Crown in 1689. It is here that one could argue the first steps to change the nature of monarchy were taken. William and Mary were given the Declaration of Rights. This clarified the rights and liberties of subjects, and of Parliament, including frequent Parliament sessions and freedom of speech, which it said was taken from them by the last Stuart monarchs. The Bill of Rights changed the power of the monarchy and its relationship with Parliament by the nature of its demands; frequent Parliaments, not declaring war without Parliamentary consent, and no royal ministerial appointees. Despite this, some powers of the Crown remained, including rights to veto legislation, and the length that Parliament convened. There are many other rules but the spirit of the Act is more important than the content. Parliament was making more demands, marking a new constitutional era.

Documents like the Declaration of Rights, later cemented as the Bill of Rights, have had a long-term effect on Britain's history. It was a landmark document relating to the civil liberties of the nation. The differences between the Declaration, and the Bill, are key when high-lighting the changing nature of the monarchy at this historical junction. Here is evidence that William is not responsible for that change, but Parliament itself. The Bill added two major changes: the first banning Catholic succession, even through marriage, forced any future monarch to take the Test Act and curtailed the King's dispensing powers; the latter putting the monarch under the law as opposed to above it. Parliament had increased its powers whilst the monarchy had reduced theirs. William's responsibility is only partial. The new monarch's recognition of Parliament's power was more clearly stated in the revised oath written by Parliament for the coronation in April 1689. William III and Mary II had to swear to govern according to 'the statutes in Parliament agreed on' instead of by 'the laws and customs . . . granted by the Kings of England', signalling a new power distribution. Once William was proclaimed King, a number of issues affected the way he ruled, and in turn had a bearing on the nature of the monarchy. It can be argued that William's co-operation with Parliament contributed to a new style of kingship through his conformity to the Bill of Rights and later Act of Settlement. His agreement to come to England at all makes him partially responsible for events. For that, his motivation plays a part too. In 1689, the subject of divine right was still being discussed. The acceptance of the doctrine had a bearing on the nature of William's reign. Most of the clergy continued to preach. Many people treated the doctrine as axiomatic. But Van der Kiste, in *Heroes of the Glorious Revolution, William & Mary*, argues that as soon as the Whig party proposed William as King, it created a sovereign who had been elected, which got rid of the principal of the divine right. In short, had the revolution created a new king or a new kingship? The Convention Parliament's method of making a decision had surely created a new style of kingship, without divine right. Jeremy Paxman, in *On Royalty*, says the wording of the coronation oath changed the nature of the monarchy, in that it also changed its tone on divine right, making the idea of ruling by God's command as preposterous, and a king or queen now had to show examples of doing good work. Meanwhile, the revisionist theory goes against the more common view that events helped steer the monarchy away from absolutism to one with more limited powers, and suggests there is actually not enough evidence to show resistance to the Crown. Some historians have closely examined the differences between abdication, fleeing and contract in the Glorious Revolution, in relation to James II vanishing, and how those words were understood in the Seventeenth Century. The most probable reason for William's agreement to come to England was to gain command of her army to boost his own anti-French alliance, without relinquishing any royal powers though. William A. Speck argues in

Redefining William III: The Impact of the King-Stadholder in its International Context, that this gave his subjects a bargaining factor to take power from him. William, as Captain-General of the Dutch Republic, had forged a Grand Alliance against France, and had already defended his own territory against Louis XIV in 1672. William did want to keep some of his prerogatives though. Both William and Mary had to agree to govern according to the statutes agreed in Parliament and to keep it in agreement over war funding. Tim Harris in *Revolution* explains that it was the issue of warfare that enabled further political reform, because in 1694 William agreed to the Triennial Act, agreeing the frequency and length of Parliament. It was in his interests to have a regular Parliament to vote in favour of financing his war against Louis XIV. The issue of the standing army affected how William ruled his kingdoms as well. This issue had also been a problem for James II before him. In the third session of the third Parliament in 1697 this was brought to attention. The issued highlighted how monarchy and Parliament were now working, with increased power to the latter. The monarchy eventually lost the authority to hold a standing army under William's reign. William's defeat on this matter had a profound effect on altering the balance of military power from the monarchy in favour of Parliament. William was often away at war, which helped create the growth of parliamentary government and cabinet decisions without him. He lost further powers as he bargained with parliament to finance his war with France. During the 1690s he lost the right to declare war, for example, as well as summon Parliament and dismiss ministers. His agreement to the Triennial Act in 1694 further ebbed away at his royal prerogative. William's inability to give the country an heir, created further problems, particularly in the matter of Protestant succession. The result was the Act of Settlement 1701, another Parliamentary Act which shaped the powers and duties of future monarchies. Such were the demands of the Act of Settlement, that the nature of Britain's monarchy was redefined forever. The development of the 'British Constitution' between the Bill of Rights (1689) and the Act of Settlement (1701) was immense. The Act of Settlement was really to lay down the rules for House of Hanover which was most likely to take over through the Protestant line of Sophia and George. Long term, the Act stopped Catholics from ever taking the throne, further reducing the power of future royals. It can be argued that there is reasonable evidence, as seen, to show that the Glorious Revolution did change the relationship between monarchy and Parliament and the nature of the monarchy per se. It was a major but gradual shift in power away from the monarchy towards Parliament. William III cannot be blamed for a re-styling of 'Britain's Constitution' and the entire nature of monarchy. It was a series of events that led to it, such as the Bill of Rights, Triennial Act and Act of Settlement. The latter has remained a contentious issue, with a number of politicians over the last few years, voicing opposition to its discriminatory content. Some describe the Act of Settlement as defining Britain. Others call it discriminatory and bigoted. In a recent House of Lords debate on the future of the Act, Baroness Buscombe said changing it would damage the tapestry of the constitution.

QUEEN ANNE
b.1665 d.1714
Reigned: 1702–1714

Queen Anne's brother-in-law and her sister Mary had ruled as joint monarchs (as opposed to King and Queen or Queen and Regent, for example) Mary II died first, her husband William III ruled alone until 1702. Mary's sister Anne then took the throne until her death in 1714, which ended the Stuart dynasty as she left no surviving children.

Anne's character has been portrayed as a tea-drinking, social nonentity with lesbian tendencies, although that is now in dispute. In 1683 Anne married Prince George of Denmark. She was pregnant 18 times, only giving birth to five babies who were alive, but all died as children. Queen Anne of Scotland was the last monarch to sit on the throne of an independent Scotland. She urged for the union of Scotland and England which happened in 1707. Ireland joined the union in 1801. Although recognised by Scotland's Parliament, as their rightful Queen, she did not have a coronation in Scotland. She had little knowledge of Scotland, and only visited the country once. She has been quoted as calling Scottish people 'strange people'. She did give Scotland much thought, according to the website *highlanderweb.co.uk*. Her vision of a United Kingdom, and the signing of the Act of Union in 1707, saw an end to Scotland's independence. Some would say that Anne's key role in losing Scotland its independence was scandal enough. But there was another side to Anne's reign that falls under the scandal category. Although she fulfilled her dynastical duties; married and tried to produce an heir, it wasn't men she was interested in at all. Scandalous for the day, she was a lesbian. She also had a fondness of spirits which earned her the nickname Brandy Nan. Diana Osen suggests this may have been a way to drown her sorrows over her disastrous pregnancies and the death of her only surviving child at the age of 11.

Anne found comfort and joy in the arms of Sarah Churchill and was apparently infatuated with her. She has been described as stronger, and more powerful, than any king's mistress throughout history. But Sarah, married to the Earl and later titled Duke of Marlborough, got too big for her boots. Her disrespect for the Queen became evident and evermore public. She became unpopular, and it's believed her enemies put a young woman called Abigail Masham into the royal service, as a lady-in-waiting of the Queen. The plan worked well. Eventually Anne fell for Abigail and started a lesbian affair. She had a gentle and pleasing character, the complete opposite to Sarah Churchill, whom the Queen decided to dismiss from her services.

Anne's health deteriorated and the different political parties were split over the problem of succession. Some were united behind the Hanover family although Anne had banned any Hanoverian coming to Britain after the future George I had visited England to ask for her hand in marriage, and changed his mind at the last minute. When she died, in 1714 of gout, alcoholism and blood disease, the majority supported the new George I from Hanover.

GEORGE I
b.1660 d.1727
Reigned: 1714–1727

Despite conceiving many times during her lifetime, Queen Anne died childless in 1714 at Kensington Palace, aged just 49. Her children were either still born or had died young. The country was, by now, mainly Protestant and the 1701 Act of Settlement ensured Britain would never again be ruled by a Catholic monarch. It was therefore decided that George, the Protestant Elector of Hanover, should become King George I. His mother had been declared next in line to the throne but had died in 1714. In Jeremy Paxman's *On Royalty*, he points out there were 57 people with a better claim to the throne than George, but that politics had become more important than blood ties. Of course, the fact that George was not a Roman Catholic was crucial. The new German King did not have much in his favour though. Somerset-Fry's *Kings and Queens* says George had to rely on trusted advisors, and that he had little knowledge of the navy or merchant sailors, and limited knowledge on the workings of government.

Britain's democracy as we know it may have turned out very differently if George had not been invited to take the throne, followed by his son and great-grandson George II and George III. Under these three monarchs, the power of the monarchy continued to disappear. Of course it also happened under William III earlier, and there are examples of it in monarchs before him. George seemed more interested in German affairs and was often absent from government meetings, perhaps because of his lack of English language skills. A senior minister would take his place.

George was a scandalous man from the start. He arrived in London with two of his mistresses and left behind another, who was a married woman, and whom he'd got pregnant. His two mistresses arriving in Britain with him were an odd sight. One was tall and slim. The other was short and very fat. They earned themselves the nickname 'the maypole and the elephant'. On top of all this, George liked to keep things in the family, and shared a mistress with his father. His poor long suffering wife Princess Sophia Dorothea had been left behind in Hanover. After 12 years she decided to have a bit of extra carnal fun herself. She took her own lover, in the form of a good looking and dashing Swedish soldier. Word soon got back to George in England though and he was very unhappy. He had the soldier killed and buried under Sophia's floorboards as a sick reminder of what had happened to him. She was then imprisoned in Ahlden Castle for the next 32 years. She died there in 1726. George took much persuasion to even allow her a proper burial. It was only the warnings from a fortune-teller that spurred him into action. George was told that he would die very soon unless he agreed for her to be buried. George therefore went to her burial in Hanover in 1727, where he died of a stroke.

The biggest scandal of George's reign was the South Sea Bubble. In 1711 a company was set up to trade with the islands of the South Seas and South America. It was all about issuing shares, keeping up confidence, selling more shares, making a profit and hoping share prices would continue to grow. The King became the company's governor in 1718, making himself a tidy profit from his own shares. But after a period of prosperity and profit, thousands lost their money when the bubble burst and the monarchy and government were engulfed in scandal. There were riots in the streets and the royal procession came under attack. King George was preparing to mobilise his troops in Hanover when things died down and the economy stabilised, partly because just as many people had 'made' money from the venture as had 'lost' it.

GEORGE II
b.1683 d.1760
Reigned: 1727–1760

Most of history's kings had affairs, mistresses and concubines. Look at Ming Huang with his forty thousand concubines. It's a wonder he had the energy to run a bath, never mind a country. However, when it comes to King George II, his sheer arrogance over his mistresses is staggering. His private agreement with his wife Caroline of Ansbach is enough to have the eyebrows raised in any swingers' club. Randy George had plenty of mistresses, and it was his wife who lined them up and chose the best looking ones for him. In a weird arrangement, Caroline chose her husband's mistresses, to make sure they were all ugly, and not as good looking as her. Mrs Henriette Howard was George's main mistress. George visited her most nights and she was pensioned off handsomely when he got fed up. In 1735, he enjoyed the company of his mistress, Amelia Sophia von Walmoden, so much that he wrote to his wife and told her how charming she was! The following year Amelia gave birth to George's son.

In November 1737 Caroline died after a painful illness. The King hovered round her deathbed, offering advice and protesting undying devotion. It was here that his famous response came when she called on him to marry again. He cried, 'Non, non, j'aurai des maîtresses.' He promised her he would only ever take mistresses; such a magnanimous gesture.

King George II died at Kensington Palace on 25 October 1760, at seven o'clock in the morning. He was 77 and had been growing increasingly blind and deaf. He was buried at Westminster Abbey on 11 November. His grandson (also George) succeeded him in 1760, after his son Frederick was killed by a cricket ball hitting him in the chest during a game. Henrietta, George II's former mistress bought land with her pay-off and built the impressive Marble Hill House in Twickenham for her retirement, which is still there.

CATHERINE THE GREAT OF RUSSIA
(OR CATHERINE II)
b.1729 d.1796
Empress of Russia 1762–1796

Catherine II was born Sophia Augusta Frederica, in a region that is now part of Poland. At the age of 15 she was sent to Russia at the invitation of the Empress Elizabeth. The point was to greet the heir to the throne, the young Grand Duke Peter. Soon after the meeting Catherine converted to the Russian Orthodox faith. Catherine and the Grand Duke Peter were married in 1745.

She took the reins of power after her husband Peter III was deposed in a coup d'etat. Catherine took part in the coup, and was claimed as Empress by her supporters (in their thousands). Peter was killed soon after and it is unclear whether Catherine played a part in his death or not. Apart from increasing the power of the rich landowners, and ignoring the plight of peasants and serfs, her main scandal was her astonishing love life. Her countless affairs were the talk of many a European royal court. She shocked others with the ages and numbers of lovers she took. After she was bored of each one, they were given lands and a pension. A series of lovers were rewarded with high-ranking jobs. One of her lovers was called Grigori Alexandrovich Potemkin and he was given a strange job after she had got bored with him and finished with him in 1776. His job was to select new lovers that were good looking and intelligent. Another lover got the usual land and pension when he was dumped, as well as four thousand peasants. Her last lover was a real toy boy, some 40 years younger than her! She claimed her son Paul was fathered by her lover Sergey Saltykov, because her husband Peter had been more interested in playing with his toy soldiers at bedtime than with her! Catherine also had an illegitimate son by another lover. In her memoirs she complained that Peter had paid attention to every other woman except her, and that she needed to receive affections in return. Joan Haslip's *Catherine the Great* explains about Peter's physical problems that made him turn his marital bed into a toy soldiers' playground. He often made her play soldiers with him as well! He would rather drink beer with the guards than make love to his pretty young wife, which is what he was doing on his wedding night as she laid waiting patiently in her new nightgown. As Haslip puts it, the Emperor needed a little operation that could have been performed by a doctor or a Rabbi! But Peter was too scared to undergo the procedure. It would have been a simple circumcision, which various cultures had been doing successfully for years. Peter however, thought there was no cure for his little obstacle. Eventually he did have an operation, but instead chose a string of mistresses over his wife, and dangled them in front of her as well. Catherine lost her virginity eight years after her wedding night, to a handsome young soldier. A note for the more serious historians, in *Catherine the Great*, Mark Raeff says too much has been written about Catherine's love life and much of it spiced up, and her political accomplishments have not been as well illuminated. She directed the expansion and modernisation of the Russian Empire, making it stronger and seen as a great power, by expanding its borders. Her achievements are worthy of several books in their own right. There are three books recommended for further reading that look at Catherine's political achievements and working life in greater depth. They are by Marc Raeff, Joan Haslip and John T Alexander.

Peter was unpopular, and Catherine's dignified silence when he treated her badly had won her much public and political sympathy and support. She had growing support from the army and the establishment.

HER QUOTES ARE AS LEGENDARY AS HER LOVE LIFE:
1. If Russians knew how to read, they would write me off.
2. I praise loudly, I blame softly.
3. I shall be an autocrat, that is my trade; and that good Lord will forgive me, that is his.
4. The more a man knows, the more he forgives.

She has been described in many ways; corrupt, complex, very sensual, a genius, having splendour, and being a nymphomaniac. Indeed there was a long line of male lovers, many much younger as she grew older. Followers tried to work out if her choice of lovers had any political implications. Meanwhile critics thought she made a bad example for other women.

In John T. Alexander's *Catherine the Great* he says almost two hundred years after her death, she is still recognised as a celebrity and a sex symbol. Historians strongly deny that there is any evidence Catherine died trying to have sex with a horse, labelling it as a myth!

THE QUEEN CAROLINE AFFAIR

QUEEN CONSORT OF GEORGE IV OF THE UNITED KINGDOM 1820–1821
b.1768 d.1821
m.1795

Caroline of Brunswick and King George III's eldest son, George Prince of Wales, got married in 1795. George was deeply in debt and was forced to marry Parliament's choice of princess, for financial and political reasons. He had previously married a Catholic girl called Maria Fitzherbert in secret, as it was against the law. He was then forced to have the marriage annulled so that he could wed Caroline, who was chosen for him by Parliament. She was 26 years old, and not into washing much. Her clothes and body were rather smelly. The Prince of Wales was not too impressed by this when he went to meet her at St James's Palace. Other reports say she dressed badly, was a rough speaker and not very bright; in all, not much going for her really. She has also been described as short, fat and ugly. Michael Farquhar calls her a foul-smelling exhibitionist.

King George III was adamant that his son would marry this smelly wretch, convinced it was an ideal match for the family. The Prince's mother, Queen Charlotte, was not so convinced. She was overruled and the wedding went ahead on the 8 April 1795. Despite the array of farm-like smells, George had held his nose and his stomach long enough to consummate the marriage. The couple had a daughter called Charlotte the following year.

By 1798 the prince and stinky Caroline were living separate lives. He had started to drink a fair bit to help him tolerate her presence. Caroline moved to Montague House in Blackheath and developed a rowdy and boisterous court round her, along with many regular male visitors. There were stories of naughty parties with lots of flesh on show. There was also a rumour that Caroline had given birth to an illegitimate son. King George III was angry about her liaison with several other men, but the public just loved her all the more. They felt a little sorry for Caroline because the Prince of Wales had pushed her aside because he wanted to see his mistress, a Catholic girl he had dated before and had wanted to marry.

Meanwhile, rumours about scandalous behaviour and raucous events at Montague House began to circulate. A Royal Commission in 1805 cleared Caroline of adultery however it did question her behaviour, and whether or not it was appropriate. This became known as the 'Delicate Investigation'. It was quite a scandal of the day, acquitting Caroline of the charges against her, but exposing her sordid life to the public, although most of it was probably untrue. The popularity of the fun-loving royal girl had started to wane and her reputation was shattered by the Delicate Investigation. It did not result in the Prince of Wales getting enough evidence to get rid of his wife altogether though. *homehistory.co.uk* says the investigation damaged the Prince's reputation too because the public thought him two-faced for revealing his wife's behaviour when his own was nothing to write home about.

Years later, Caroline decided to head to Europe and employed Bartolomeo Pergami as her secretary. But, although she wanted to make a clean break from scandal, stories soon reached London of her affair, dressing to show the flesh, and behaving inappropriately. In England, on the 29 January 1820, King George III died and his son the Prince of Wales now became King George IV. Caroline was now Queen Consort, which caused many worries. The new King George IV needed a speedy divorce to get rid of Caroline. To save himself from a public divorce and from having his dirty linen washed in public, the new King had already agreed to pay her off in return for getting out of Britain, staying out, and not becoming Queen. Caroline liked to be awkward and so came back from Europe in 1820, to be met by cheering crowds. Parliament had already been debating her behaviour abroad to try and discredit her. They had wanted to legally remove Caroline from being Queen, by the legal voiding of their marriage. Here the future Queen of England had been on trial for her own position and title. The proceedings lasted for 11 weeks in total and were centred around Caroline's alleged affair with Pergami. The King's personal life and his mistresses were all kept out of the hearing.

All judges, peers and bishops were ordered to attend the hearing, and Caroline herself. In relation to witnesses giving so called evidence to the hearing, the author of *A Queen on Trial*, A. E. Smith, talks about unconvincing performers. Supporters of Caroline claimed the allegations were exaggerated or made up. Smith argues many of Caroline's own witnesses were not very impressive either. At the end of the investigation, the Bill did not get enough votes to go through. Therefore, Caroline was triumphant. The trial had been detailed in every newspaper for weeks, filling every element of social chatter from cartoons to public bars and work places to cartoon strips. Even graffiti daubed on the walls of cities.

George IV's coronation was set for July 1821. George did not invite his own Queen and was worried she would turn up and cause a scene. She did turn up at Westminster to see the new King and the crowd turned against Caroline. They booed her and she fled. Caroline died soon after.

WILLIAM IV
b.1765 d.1837
Reigned: 1830–1837

Best known for his affair with Mrs Jordan, 10 illegitimate children and rambling speeches, King William IV was the unexpected King. He was the third child of King George III and Queen Charlotte. His two older brothers died, making him the next king at the age of 64. He lived a relatively quiet life as the Duke of Clarence with Mrs Jordan for 20 years. He did however have a distinguished and successful naval career. The couple had five sons and five daughters, nine of which were the Duke's. She was an actress, real name Dorothea Bland, but called Mrs Jordan to explain her pregnancies. The affair, although they lived together at Bushy House, ended acrimoniously in 1811. There were disagreements over her financial settlement. She received £4,400 per year and custody of the daughters, as long as she gave up acting. When she went back on the agreement because she needed to earn some extra money, the Duke took custody of the daughters and stopped paying some of the maintenance. She fled to Paris where she died broke in 1816.

In 1818 William married Princess Adelaide of Saxe-Meiningen. They spent almost 20 years together, until his death. She also helped sort out his growing financial crisis and crippling debts. He was known to often walk unaccompanied through the streets of London, and was popular in the early part of his reign. He hated the pomp associated with being King. He even tried to give away Buckingham Palace to the army, as a barracks, and also to Parliament after it burned down in 1834. He cut back on the number of horses he had and gave away many royal paintings. He was known for making impromptu, rambling speeches.

SUMMARY

William, then Duke of Clarence, deserted his partner of 20 years in return for money. There was a succession crisis (again) when his brother's only child, Princess Charlotte died in childbirth.

englishmonarchs.co.uk notes that Parliament offered to pay off the Duke's debts if he married and secured the succession. William deserted Mrs Jordan without qualms. Nice man! Living in sin with his partner for so long and having so many illegitimate children was only a minor scandal, if at all. It was all the other smaller things that added up. He did act rather strangely, offering strangers a lift in the royal carriage, spitting in public and constantly bowing to his subjects.

QUEEN VICTORIA AND HER MEN

QUEEN OF THE UNITED KINGDOM OF GREAT BRITAIN AND IRELAND & EMPRESS OF INDIA
b.1819 d.1901
Reigned: 1837–1901

Queen Victoria was actually called Alexandrina Victoria and she holds the record as the longest serving monarch in British history (so far). She was born in Kensington Palace in 1819. This period in history is called the Victorian period. It was a time of great discovery and developments in science, politics, architecture, industry and military matters. Her reign is synonymous with the expansion of the British Empire and its global supreme power. Victoria was of mostly German descent, the granddaughter of King George III. She was the first monarch to use Buckingham Palace as her official residence. She earned herself the nickname 'the grandmother of Europe', having more than 40 grandchildren across Europe. By arranging marriages between some of them she managed diplomatically to tie together many of the royal houses, governments and countries. But there was plenty of scandal dominating the Victorian years, starting just before her reign, and carrying on right through to the next century.

WHO'S THE DADDY?
Just as there were serious doubts over the possible illegitimacy of King Edward IV, there have also been raised eyebrows over the possible illegitimacy of the mighty Queen Victoria. The young Victoria was bound up in cotton wool as a girl, not allowed to play outside, helped down the stairs, and had her food tasted for poison; all because if she died before producing an heir, it could spell the end of the monarchy as there were no suitable or close enough members of the family to take up the crown. Queen Victoria's biographer A. N. Wilson wrote an article on Mail Online (4 March

2009) which said the threats to the young Victoria's life early on in her reign may have ended the royal line of succession, as the crown would have passed to Ernest Augustus Duke of Cumberland, later King of Hanover.

The young Victoria's household was run by Sir John Conroy. Later in life, she confessed that the reason she hated Conroy was because she had witnessed the Irish soldier and her mother being 'familiar'. There are a number of medical questions that also come to light which makes us wonder if Sir John Conroy really was Victoria's father. Her grandfather King George III had suffered from porphyria. This nasty disease does all manner of things to you such as discolour your urine, make your skin itchy and send you mad. The madness of King George is notorious, but the condition is also hereditary. It stops at Queen Victoria, suggesting a new male gene perhaps? Another question has to be asked about the haemophiliac gene which seems to start with Queen Victoria, not before. Does this come from Sir John Conroy? It has infected several of Victoria's descendants.

This is the evidence that stacks up against Sir John Conroy being Victoria's real father. It is far from conclusive but there are certainly enough questions raised. If Victoria was illegitimate it proves the point made when raising the possibility of King Edward IV's illegitimacy, i.e. it must have happened several times in twelve hundred years of one family, queens bearing another man's child on the quiet, children conceived before their parents' wedding vows etc. This brings into question the whole legitimacy of the royal family. One could argue none of them should be there, that the whole system is a scandal.

LADY FLORA HASTINGS

Another scandal of the Victorian era caused the Queen to be booed in public and have eggs thrown at her royal coach. It was a time when even a rumour of bad behaviour could ruin a lady's good name. This scandal centred round Lady Flora Hastings, a former lady-in-waiting to Victoria's mother. In January 1839, 18 months after Victoria had come to the throne, Lady Flora had visited family in Scotland, and had been complaining of stomach pains. Sir John Conroy had accompanied her on that trip. Flora was unwell and suffering from cancer, although that wasn't known at the time. She had a badly swollen abdomen. Queen Victoria, who often referred to Conroy as 'the devil', accused Flora of being pregnant by him. Lady Flora's reputation was shattered. She had to undergo a painful medical examination to prove she was not with child. Arguments involved the Queen, Flora's family, and politicians. It was all played out in the press and public sympathy was with the dying Lady Flora Hastings, not Queen Victoria. As the *Irish Times* put it, 'it was a scandal that rocked court and government and caused Victoria's popularity to plummet. It involved sex, high politics, personal tragedy and a terrible injustice to an innocent woman.'

QUEEN VICTORIA IN MOURNING

Queen Victoria spent years as a grieving widow following the death of her husband, Prince Albert. His full name and title was Prince Albert of Saxe-Coburg and Gotha, and Francis Albert Augustus Charles Emmanuel. He lived from 1819 to 1861. Prim and proper Victorian attitudes to sex and controversy were more his ideals than hers. He married Victoria when he was 20 and they had nine children. He was 42 when he died. Victoria was absent from public life for many years. After the lengthy period of mourning, following the death of her husband, Victoria started to come out of her self-inflicted shell of pity. It was attributed to her close relationship with her personal servant John Brown, who had also served Prince Albert. In 1866 Victoria attended the state opening of Parliament, the first time since her beloved Prince Albert had passed away. She had slowly started to fulfil her public duties, with much relief from palace officials and politicians who had been trying to persuade her to come out of the shadows for years.

A newspaper in Switzerland claimed Victoria and John Brown had married in secret and that she was expecting their first child together. There were some cheeky and bold claims in Britain as well. *Punch* magazine gave her the nickname Mrs Brown and the name has stuck ever since. In 2005, Judi Dench played Queen Victoria in a film, alongside Billy Connolly as John Brown. The title of that film was *Mrs Brown*. Republicans seized the chance to play politics with the situation, criticising her for withdrawing from public life. John Brown was blamed by some for her disappearance. A pamphlet was published which claimed the Queen and Brown had joined together in a morganatic marriage, i.e. none of her titles or possessions would pass to the partner of a lower rank, or their descendants.

What we cannot be totally sure about is whether or not the relationship between Victoria and Brown was platonic or whether it was a full blown sexual partnership. As history is always about facts, rather than speculation, what we can report on is the mood of the nation and the calls for the Queen to come out of hiding. There was already a strong anti-monarchy feeling sweeping the country. Republicanism had swept across mainland Europe. Queen Victoria blindly carried on in her own sweet way, refusing to do anything she did not want to do.

She even published her own book dedicated to John Brown entitled, *More Leaves from the Journal of a Life in the Highlands*. In Rowan Wilson's *World Famous Royal Scandals* he argues the scandal surrounding Victoria and John Brown reached such proportions in the 1860s that there were real fears for the future of the monarchy in Britain. John Brown died at the age of 56, in 1883, and lay in state for six days. His death was almost treated in the same manner as a royal when it was reported in the Court Circular. In Nigel Cawthorne's *Royal Scandals* he says Brown's obituary was longer than Disraeli's. Upon orders from Victoria herself, his rooms were to be left untouched, just like Albert's. After Victoria's death in 1901, her son King Edward VII still hated the fiery Scot with a passion, and arguably as a mark of disrespect, turned Brown's apartment at Windsor Castle into a billiards room and ordered statues and busts of the man to be removed, including the one from the hallway at Balmoral, and all his mother's private photos of him were also to be burned.

MUNSHI THE MAN

Having a series of partners is by no means a scandal these days, but for Queen Victoria, that's how it seemed to be for many. Therefore, there was a mixed reaction to the Queen taking up another companion after the death of John Brown. She turned to Munshi Hafir Abdul Karim. By now she was in her sixties and 'Munshi' as she called him, was only in his twenties. There were more than a few raised eyebrows at the 'special' relationship they had. She was so fond of him he was given his own staff and a cottage at Windsor. But it was not only their close relationship, in normal terms, that was causing concerns. The biggest gossip was that Munshi was a spy! How racist it is these days, but her advisors warned her against the unsuitability of having a relationship with a dark-skinned man! Edward VII tried to get rid of traces of Munshi as he did with Brown, after the death of his mother, and had all of Munshi's private papers burned. One wonders now if there was some inappropriate secret written down in

Munshi's papers; something that could have rocked the monarchy. Sadly, for historians, that's something we will never know.

THE CLEVELAND STREET SCANDAL

Scandal surrounded Victoria's extended family too and in July 1889 a male brothel was found to be operating at an address in London. The names of the customers became of particular interest to the press and everybody else for that matter. The brothel was operating at a house in Cleveland Street, in London.

The newspapers insinuated that prominent aristocrats, including Lord Arthur Somerset, head of the Prince of Wales's stables, and Prince Albert Victor, Queen Victoria's grandson, were regular and frequent customers to the premises. What made the scandal much worse were allegations of a government cover-up over who was using the premises. There were allegations that 'distinguished' gentlemen were using the brothel, but because of their position, were having their identities withheld from the general public.

The scandal put homosexuality into a bad light. At the time, it was seen as aristocratic men corrupting young working-class youths. This was not a time known for its sexual tolerance. It was in fact all happening in a period of national abhorrence for homosexuality, which saw the sensational trials of Oscar Wilde in 1895. At the time, sexual acts between men were illegal in Britain, and the brothel's clients faced almost certain prosecution.

One of the clients, Lord Arthur Somerset, the equerry to the Prince of Wales, and the brothel keeper, Charles Hammond, managed to flee abroad. The rent boys in question worked as messenger boys for the local Post Office. They were taken to court where they received light sentences. No clients were actually prosecuted over the scandal. Henry FitzRoy, Earl of Euston, was named in the press as a client, but he successfully sued the paper for libel. The British press never named Prince Albert Victor, and there is no evidence he ever visited the brothel. But the rumours that he frequented the premises did the rounds. This was a major scandal of the day; Prince Eddy (as he was known) mixing with rent boys – according to the gossip.

It all began in July 1889 when Police Constable Luke Hanks was investigating a theft from the London Central Telegraph Office. During the investigation, a 15-year-old telegraph boy named Charles Thomas Swinscow had quite a bit of money on him, about 14 shillings in total. This was the equivalent to several weeks' wages in his pockets. At the time, messenger boys were not allowed to carry any personal cash at work, to prevent their own money being mixed up with customer's money. The boy immediately became a suspect in the theft. Constable Hanks took him to the police station for questioning. Swinscow must have been scared by the experience because under arrest he told all. He admitted earning the money whilst working as a rent boy for a man called Charles Hammond and said that Hammond operated a brothel at 19 Cleveland Street. According to Swinscow, he was introduced to Hammond by a General Post Office clerk called Henry Newlove: he also named two 17-year-old boys who also worked at the brothel. Constable Hanks obtained statements from both of these boys as well.

At this point the case was handed over to Detective Inspector Frederick Abberline. Inspector Abberline went to the brothel on 6 July to arrest Hammond and Newlove for violation of Section II of the Criminal Law Amendment Act 1885. But he arrived too late; Hammond and Newlove had escaped and the house was all locked up. The brothel had closed down. Abberline did not give up though for he tracked down and arrested Newlove at his mother's house nearby. Newlove then went on to name Lord Arthur Somerset and Henry FitzRoy, Earl of Euston, as well as an Army Colonel as regular visitors to Cleveland Street; Somerset was the Head of the Prince of Wales's Stables.

The Cleveland Street scandal was a big deal at the time, but gradually faded from public interest. The release of Public Record Office police documents in 1975 and the publication of the private letters of Lord Somerset, confirmed the involvement of the Prince in the scandal, beyond reasonable doubt. It now seems as though a cover-up and damage limitation exercise had gone on. Officially, Prince Eddy died of pneumonia in 1892. But one theory suggests he died of syphilis, while another claims that he died of a morphine overdose. One conspiracy claims he survived until the 1920s in an asylum, and that his death was faked. Eddy even became a suspect in the Jack the Ripper murders!

You can read more about the Cleveland Street Scandal in the follow up to this book, *The Pocket Guide to Scandals of the Aristocracy.*

Chapter Four

Scandalous Rulers
of the Twentieth Century

TIME PROGRESSED AND THE SCANDALS CONTINUED

EDWARD VII, THE HOOKERS AND THAT DIVORCE
b.1841 d.1910
Reigned: 1901–1910

Queen Victoria's son, the Prince of Wales and the future King Edward VII (1841–1910) commonly known as Bertie, was well known to love the company of prostitutes, in several countries. He got away with a lot we probably don't know about because photography was still a new thing. If a senior royal was seen leaving a well-known knocking shop today, you can guarantee there would be someone outside filming it, and getting it on *youtube.com* within the hour – and that's on top of paparazzi following the royals like a wasp follows jam or a fly follows dung. Edward could enjoy a debauch life of non-stop female entertainment, and he did.

He was known to frequent an area where prostitutes worked; Cremorne Pleasure Gardens in London. It was between Chelsea Harbour and the end of the King's Road and was at its peak of popularity between 1845 to 1877. Most of the site of the gardens is now built over. The name survives in Cremorne Road, which you can still walk down today, maybe over the precise spot where Edward was getting his wicked way with some poor innocent Victorian wench.

Edward is also known to have paid for sex in Egypt, France and Germany during his travels. Some prostitutes travelled for miles to have sex with him. In Paris his regular visits to Le Chabanais were legendary. Le Chabanais was a well-known luxury brothel in the French capital. It operated near the Louvre from the 1870s to just after the end of World War II when brothels in France were all made illegal and shut down. Today the building has been split into private apartments, but you can still see where the future king romped away many a night with a French hooker. He went there so often that one room had his coat of arms put up over one of the beds. In the same room he had a copper tub which he filled with champagne, and took many baths with various prostitutes. This extravagance should be set in the context of serious poverty and disease in the Victorian slums in places like London and Manchester, and the starving unemployed. During times of poverty and starvation in poor parts of Victorian Britain, Edward was a big fat pig. He often had five meals a day, up to 10 courses each, and a massive waistline to go with it. Meanwhile, at the club, greedy Edward had a special chair built to accommodate his taking a number of girls in various positions at the same time. The weird chair was sold at auction in 1996 to a private buyer, but a replica is on display at the Prague Sex Museum.

In 1903, such was Edward's reputation of being a playboy and his love of many girls at once at Le Chabanais, a famous cartoon appeared of him in the magazine *L'indiscret*. It showed him sat on a chair surrounded by prostitutes. Apparently he had his own special chair (separate to his love chair), which he sat on whilst the girls paraded in front of him, and he picked his favourite, or favourites. He had one prostitute, Cora Pearl, served up to him on a silver plate, with a decorative garnish. She did it for a bet, and said she was the meat nobody could cut. Cora had been through the beds of the nobility like a greedy person goes through a box of chocolates. She loved to help them spend their money and charged up to a thousand pounds a night (in the 1800s)! It's not clear how much Edward paid for having sex with her. Cora's real name was Emma Elizabeth Crouch, born in the 1830s. She had affairs with a number of European dukes and princes. Edward had a brief fling with a woman called Hortense Schneider. All but a hooker in name, she was known to let any noble or royal man have sex with her, which earned her the strange and stomach-churning nickname of Le Passage des Princes! Schneider was the subject of the film *La Valse de Paris* (1950).

In England Edward was known to have entertained countless prostitutes from his quarters at the Cavendish Hotel, Jermyn Street, in London. The hotel is still there today. Edward's poor wife, Princess Alexandra, knew about his hookers and other affairs he had, and kept a dignified silence. Edward was involved in a few messy divorces and was even summonsed to court in one hearing, where a married woman he had an affair with, had produced a child by a third man and pleaded insanity so her husband could not divorce her. This was perhaps the most famous of Edward's scandals, which saw him in the dock. It was 1870, and when asked, Edward told the court that there had been no improper familiarity between the woman, Harriet Mordaunt, and himself. The future King of the country, lied to the court; royal perjury at its best. His mother Queen Victoria had tried so hard to get him out of testifying; he obviously had a lot to hide, and tried to hide behind his mummy's skirt. Mordaunt, although listing some of the men she had had an affair with, simply added 'others' to the list. We assume this included the Prince, as Mordaunt had admitted an affair with him to her own husband. We also know a few of Edward's friends had also been with her. Soon after the trial, Edward was booed in public wherever he went, and there were serious calls for the abolition of the monarchy. This was front page news and a massive scandal in its time. Cartoons appeared in the press making a complete mockery of Edward and his wicked ways. Edward had let his trousers rule his brain, and rocked the monarchy to its foundation. He did not learn from his errors, and carried on with his affairs.

THE BACCARAT SCANDAL

Edward VII was also at the centre of yet another scandal, when he was still just the Prince of Wales. This time it was all about cheating at cards. Perhaps not a huge scandal by today's standards, but in 1890 it was the scandal of the decade. It was September, during St Leger Week at Doncaster Races. The centre of the event was at a party in a house near Hull. The Prince was the guest of honour at the bash. Sir William Gordon-Cumming was there too, and the guests played baccarat, an illegal gambling game known to be one of the Prince's favourites. Although it was illegal it was still a favourite pursuit of the rich at many a society party. Some of the players that night accused Sir William of cheating. They said he had changed the size of his bets on the table after winning or losing a hand. There was a second night of playing, when the guests teamed up to watch him closely. Sir William had won more than £200 over both days. He was accused by his mistress's husband, perhaps as an act of revenge.

The guests told the Prince what they had noticed and then decided to confront Sir William, who denied it all. Sir William agreed to sign a contract stating he would never play cards again in exchange for the scandal to be kept secret. But word got out in Sir William's circle of friends and he was furious one side of the bargain had not been kept. He decided to sue those who had accused him of cheating, for deformation of character. The Prince of Wales was called to court as a witness because he had been playing the illegal game and had not reported the activity to the appropriate authorities.

Sir William lost his case, was fired from the army, retired to his country estate in Scotland, married his fiancée and had four children. He never mixed in the higher circles of society again and remained bitter over what had happened. The letter he had signed promising never to play cards again was a key part of his downfall. He told the court he had only signed it to keep the incident quiet, so as not to bring the Prince's name into disrepute.

Sir William said he lost all of his friends during the court case. When he moved to Scotland he surrounded himself with new friends and lots of noisy house parties, much to his wife's annoyance. Havers, Grayson and Shankland's *The Royal Baccarat Scandal* said Sir William's life had been centred round being a soldier and that his life had no purpose after he had been discharged because of the scandal. Then when the chance to clear his name vanished he became empty of purpose. They asked, when a man's heart is in the army and in society, and both are taken from him, what effect it has on his family. His daughter Elma is quoted in the book, talking about the effect the royal baccarat scandal had on her father and the family. Elma Napier, nee Gordon-Cumming, died in 1973. To this day we do not know if Sir William was guilty or not, or whether he really did sign the 'confession' to keep the Prince of Wales's name out of the scandal.

TSAR NICHOLAS II
b.1868 d.1918
Ruled from 1894–1917
Assassinated

As we have discovered scandals are not confined to just one country and can hit any nation, Russia being no exception to this. Nicholas was the last in the line of Russian Tsars, their equivalent to king. His gruesome death and that of his family's has created a scandalous, chilling and mysterious story to the end of the royal Russian dynasty.

It is important, and interesting, to look briefly at how power slowly ebbed away, and finally slipped right through his fingers. There is always a moment in the history of conflict and overthrow when a ruler suddenly switches from a position of authority to a position without any. It is not always a precise moment and may be the result of a number of incidents which culminate in the loss of power. Take the recent historical example of Iraqi president Saddam Hussein. When he finally went on the run, at which point did he lose control? Not an easy question to answer. It is the same with Tsar Nicholas. There were a number of situations, as in the case of the end of their power base, where some people see the leader as being in control, some start to question it, others deny it still exists.

Nicholas was deposed during the Russian Revolution. He was born Nikolai Aleksandrovich Romanov in 1868. He was the eldest son of Tsar Alexander III. He succeeded his father in 1894 and married Princess Alexandra of Hesse-Darmstadt, which was a small duchy in Germany. Together they had five children, four daughters and a son called Alexis, who had haemophilia. Nicholas was an inexperienced leader and did not trust his ministers. He made the bad decision of expansion in Manchuria, which started a war with Japan in 1904. The Russians lost this war and there was growing discontent in the country. There were a number of riots and strikes which resulted in 'Bloody Sunday' in January of 1905, where the army opened fired on a crowd in St Petersburg during a demonstration for reform.

Rasputin was a confidant of the family, and seen as having too much influence on the Tsar's wife, and the Tsar's war policies. He was murdered by a group of noblemen in 1916. The story goes that his penis was severed and stolen. Several people have since claimed possession, including those who claim to worship it as a fertility charm.

There was growing opposition to the Tsar and under pressure he granted a constitution which created a parliament. It meant the middle class had a say on elections to the 'Duma'. But Nicholas had his secret police out in force, crushing opposition on the quiet, to strengthen his own position. Changes in the law meant outspoken radicals were not allowed to be elected. Nicholas took direct control of the Russian Army and was directly blamed for all its losses in World War I from 1914 onwards, and it suffered many heavy losses after a number of poor military decisions. During the war inflation was up and there was a shortage of food. Russian people were enduring terrible poverty, they were hungry and unhappy.

In February 1917, anti-Tsarist feelings escalated and there were more demonstrations. Eventually the army stopped supporting

Nicholas and there was a shift of power to a new temporary government as Nicholas abdicated. He was held captive, along with his family, in a number of locations around the country. The Tsar sought sanctuary in Britain. The Government approved, but George V (the Tsar's cousin) refused, fearing a socialist reaction in Britain. He may well have lived out his enforced retirement in a nice little chalet in the mountains, but there was another shift of power. In October 1917, the new provisional government was overthrown itself, by the Bolsheviks. There was a terrible period of civil war. In July 1918, Nicholas, and his family were all executed in a basement in Yekaterinburg, near the Ural Mountains. The leader of the Bolsheviks Vladimir Lenin did not order the execution (a disputed fact) but did not care either. They were killed by firing squad, and there was no trial.

The family's execution was a scandalous and messy affair. Not a professional firing squad that would make a quick, clean and humane killing. There were nine Red Guards, some of whom were supposed to be drunk at the time. There was a hail of ricocheting bullets. Nicholas was shot in the head first. His daughters Anastasia, Tatiana, Olga and Maria were shot and then bayoneted several times. The

Livadia Palace, Ukraine. This was the summer home of Nicholas II and his family. Today it is a museum and conference centre and attracts thousands of tourists.

bodies were burned with acid, thrown down a mine to rot, and then later put in a shallow grave 12 miles from the place of execution.

The remains of Nicholas, Alexandra and three of their children were not found until as recently as 1991. The remains of Alexei, the heir, and his sister Maria lay undiscovered in a different place until 2007. DNA tests have been carried out on all the bones and show that they belong to the Tsar and his family. Since their discovery, the bones have been reburied in the imperial resting place in St Petersburg. The family was canonised as saints by the Russian Orthodox Church in 2000. For years, descendants of the Romanovs demanded that the killings should be reclassified as premeditated murder, rather than execution. In 2008, Russia's Supreme Court declared the imperial dynasty as 'victims of political repression', over-turning a lower court ruling that classified the killings as plain murder. The ruling cleared the family of being enemies of the Russian people, which the Bolsheviks had labelled them, in order to have a reason to shoot them.

Throughout the years of the hard line Soviet Union, government propaganda called Nicholas names such as 'Bloody Nicholas', accusing him of many crimes. Since the collapse of the Soviet Union in 1991, attitudes amongst the people have changed. Interest and discussion in the Romanov dynasty has been reignited without fear of arrest. There is only a very small minority of Russians who want back their own royal family. Many are just curious about the stories colouring their history. Faithful communists still see the dynasty as a blood-thirsty, cruel, over privileged, wealthy, pompous race that is now best consigned to history.

KING ZOG I OF ALBANIA
PREVIOUSLY PRIME MINISTER AND PRESIDENT OF ALBANIA
b.1895 d.1961
Reigned 1928–1939

There is not too much scandal surrounding King Zog, but he led an interesting life. Zog was not recognised as King of Albania by many countries. This was because he was not related to any of the European royal houses, only to Arab ones. Zog attempted to unite the Christians and Muslims in his own country. He tried to build a better schooling system and a better army. In the early 1930s Mussolini liked Albania and was very supportive. But he started to interfere more and make extra demands. Eventually Italy invaded Albania. Zog and the

Parmoor where Zog's dogs patrolled the house

royal family were sent into exile. At first they stayed in The Ritz Hotel in London, after which they lived in Sunninghill in Berkshire (1941), and finally they lived at Parmoor House in Buckinghamshire. Some of his staff lived in the surrounding village of Lane End. It was Zog's huge, vicious guard dogs that became well-known in this story. Zog's armed guards patrolled the huge house and grounds to protect people from the dogs as much as anything else.

In 1946 King Zog and most of his family went to live in Egypt at the invitation of King Farouk, although Farouk was also overthrown, in 1952. Zog made his final choice of home as France. He died at the age of 65 and was buried in the French capital, Paris. His son Leka was pronounced H M King Leka of the Albanians by the exiled Albanian community. Zog's widow died almost 50 years later, aged 87. Nobody can call Zog's life uneventful. He survived 55 assassination attempts and smoked one hundred and fifty cigarettes a day.

KING FAROUK THE PLAYBOY
b.1920 d.1965
Reigned 1936–1952

Farouk was the tenth ruler in the Muhammed Ali Dynasty, and was educated at the Royal Military Academy in Woolwich, in London. When he took the throne he was a very popular young King. At his coronation he made a public radio address to the nation. It was the first time in history that an Egyptian king had directly addressed his people:

> "If it is God's will to lay on my shoulders at such an early age the responsibility of kingship, I appreciate the duties that will be mine, and I am prepared for all sacrifices in the cause of my duty."

His words were rather meaningless though. He spent his days as King spending money like it was going out of fashion. He slept with as many women as possible. Some were in agreement, others were forced and some were paid. The penultimate king of Egypt had a fascinating and rather scandalous life and reign over his country. He had an enormous love of mistresses and prostitutes, liked to gamble, was anti-British, had a hundred red cars (banning all subjects from owning red cars), confiscated his mother's property and banned her from the country. Apparently he had very small genitals, had a huge porn collection and seduced a few under–18 girls. It's a brief but not exhaustive list of mischief in King Farouk's life, and worthy of a Hollywood blockbuster. Of course, nobody knows really how small his genitals were, except the thousands of women he slept with, or so he claimed. Some say he was also partially impotent.

He came to the throne in 1936 when he was at the tender age of 16. His reign was fully supported by the British at the time, who kept him in power. The ungrateful Farouk was quite open about hoping the Nazis would eventually kick the Brits out of his country though, which was not a wise attitude to have. His mother Queen Nazli had an affair with Farouk's teacher, and then a soldier, who she shamelessly married off to her own daughter afterwards. Nazli, her daughter and the new husband went to live in California and the women ditched Islam in favour of Catholicism. It is at this point that Farouk went mad and confiscated all her possessions and banned her from coming home. Farouk's wife, ironically called Farida (meaning the only one), had a few different lovers herself. To get revenge Farouk had a fling with his cousin's wife.

Farouk issued the droit du roi over the daughters and wives of the men in his kingdom. It is not known whether he actually took up this right and slept with female subjects as part of this legal right, or not. I would suggest he issued this to make himself look powerful, desirable and as a way of excusing his bed-hopping promiscuous behaviour, or to divert attention away from his small genitals and impotence problems. Nigel Cawthorne's *The World's Greatest Royal Scandals* says Farouk became so notorious that if there were seven deadly sins, then he would have found an eighth. Farouk was the ultimate playboy.

He was eventually overthrown and sent into exile. But he still had the taste of the good life, travelling in style with a massive entourage. The paparazzi loved him and followed him everywhere. He was the original showbiz king. Farouk was like an over-sexed Roman Emperor. Before being overthrown, he had five huge palaces, each with a harem of sexy women to see to his every need. He is known to have kidnapped, blackmailed and imprisoned women who turned him down. He had an aid that was sent out to brothels to look for beautiful light-skinned women. He had a long term affair with a Jewish girl called Irene. She wasn't that keen on him though. Apparently, the British persuaded her to hang around him to keep an eye on what he was up to. The British were nervous of his pro-Nazi stance. She moved into the palace, right next to his wife, all at the same time his other bit on the side, Fatima, was having his baby. Irene, who was seen as the real queen in Egypt, left Farouk in 1943 because he was cheating on her. During the Second World War, he upset a lot of people, because the country was in blackout at night, fearful of German and Italian bombing. But Farouk insisted on having all the lights in the palace burning all night long, putting his country at risk of being bombed.

Cawthorne has a fascinating insight into some of Farouk's parties. He says the King had a real fetish for belly dancers. He had several of them appear nude at his private parties, insisting they shaved off all their pubic hair for guests to enjoy the intimate view, and that Farouk was into corporal punishment as well. His very patient, or stupid, wife Farida finally divorced him over his infidelity. In 1949 Farouk spotted a 16-year-old girl in a jeweller's shop, and took a fancy to her. Her name was Narriman and she became his second wife. Not known for doing things by halves, Farouk had a prostitute-ridden 12-week stag do, all over Europe, and after the wedding he had a 16-week honeymoon. After his marriage he paid a team of pretty nurses to man the top floor of a local hospital round the clock for him. This was not for any ailments he had, but he turned the floor into a sex-den bachelor pad.

Farouk was supposed to be a kleptomaniac, and loved stealing or picking pockets, not for a laugh, but to genuinely steal things. He earned himself the nickname 'the Thief of Cairo'. Apparently he pinched a pocket watch from Sir Winston Churchill! Farouk was over-thrown in 1952, after a military coup, led by Muhammed Naguib and Gamal Abdel Nasser. He was forced into exile, first in Monaco, then in Italy. His son, just a baby, was proclaimed King Faud II, but Egypt was now more or less a complete republic. The monarchy was in fact completely abolished, soon after, in June 1953. Farouk's popularity in Egypt had waned over the years because his government was seen as corrupt and weak. He was blamed for not helping Palestine when it lost so much land to Israel in the Arab-Israeli war of 1948. This was really the end of the road for him. Muslims in the country thought he had badly let them down.

In exile, with his wife Narriman, he met a 16-year-old girl, Irma. Scraping the barrel of behaviour he was sending gifts and flowers to her at school! The dirty old man was in his early thirties by now and getting rather overweight. His excessive love of food and alcohol had turned the dashingly slim playboy into a rather large man of over 20 stones. He had several more mistresses, and then died at dinner clutching his throat. Some claim he was poisoned by a lover or even Egyptian intelligence officers, but this was never proved. There was never an autopsy and no inquest either. His last supper was a massive feast of oysters, fruit and vegetables. Irma, having been his 'faithful' mistress for 13 years, took pride of place at Farouk's funeral. She claims, but cannot prove, that they got married.

THE RULING ROYALS OF MONACO

THE SEVEN-HUNDRED YEAR MARITAL CURSE

The ruling Grimaldi family of Monaco has been plagued with troubles and scandals for many years. The fabled 'Curse of the Grimaldis' is said to date back to 1297, when the first Grimaldi, Francesco the Spiteful, entered the principality in disguise and killed its inhabitants. The so-called curse is supposed to prevent the family from having long and happy marriages. You get a sense of what these royals are like just by the titles of some of the books written about them. John Glatt called his book *The Ruling House of Monaco: The Story of a Tragic Dynasty* and Anne Edwards called hers, *The Grimaldis of Monaco: The Centuries of Scandal*. Edwards describes them as ambitious and hot-blooded, but is right to point out that they have survived several wars, when many other royal dynasties lost their crowns.

Prince Rainier started his reign in 1949, turning the one-time rather dull tiny Riviera principality, once accused of laundering Mafia cash, into an exciting, billionaire's glitzy playground. The change of image and fortune was partly as a result of Rainier's marriage to Hollywood actress Grace Kelly in 1956. The next few decades saw affairs, rows and bitter divorces within the wider family. Princess Grace suffered from eating disorders and miscarriages, apparently missing her Hollywood life. She is reported to have had a relationship with film director Robert Dornhelm in the 1970s, although it was never admitted. Royal biographer Robert Lacey, however, is confident this was an affair. Another affair reportedly took place in 1982, with another much younger man, head-hunter Jeffrey Fitzgerald. Royal writer Diane Osen says Princess Grace went to great lengths to shield her young lovers from the media spotlight. Princess Grace apparently felt trapped inside the palace walls and in 1981 told a worried Lady Diana Spencer not to worry too much because things would only get WORSE! Princess Grace died in a car crash in 1982, after her Rover plunged off the edge of a cliff in Monaco. Her daughter Princess Stephanie, who was a passenger, survived. It was suggested that Princess Grace had suffered a minor stroke at the wheel.

Prince Rainier's children brought scandal to the ruling family over the years. Princess Caroline appeared topless in a newspaper, after paparazzi used long lenses from the shore to snap her as she was on a boat in the Riviera. She did not give her permission and the magazine was forced to pay damages. She married a man 17 years younger, against her father's wishes. The marriage lasted just two years. She married again in 1983, but the curse struck again, and her second husband was killed in an accident in 1990. Second daughter Princess Stephanie ran away to a circus, had three children out of wedlock, and two divorces. She was the dynasty's first ever Princess to give birth outside of marriage.

PRINCE LAURENT OF BELGIUM
b.1963

Laurent is the son of Albert II of Belgium. He slipped down the succession ladder from third to eleventh, after female royals were given the same rights to succeed to the throne as men. He is also well-known for disliking royal protocol. He married a British woman in 2003 and had three children.

In 2006 the country was gripped by a serious financial scandal, with allegations that money set aside for the Belgian Navy, was diverted to funds intended to pay for work on Laurent's villa. Magistrates were quick to publicly announce that the Prince was not involved in the allegations in any way at all. Police interviewed him in 2007 and he said he had no way of knowing the funds may have been used inappropriately. Twelve other people were accused of embezzling 2.2m euros of naval money. Newspapers said 1.2m euros had not been traced. The Prince was innocent though.

Critics acknowledged the Prince's innocence in the matter, but shunned his attitude to money, and his difficulty on getting by on his royal income of 300,000 euros a month. He was accused of wasting money on extravagant clothes, watches and cars, when many people struggled to get by on their normal wages.

Chapter Five

No End in Sight!

Time seems to have done little to alleviate the scandalous ways in which some monarchs insist on behaving, and so it seems that few lessons have actually been learned. Perhaps though we should consider that their behaviour is a reflection of real life and that they are not in fact any different to other individuals except in one way, that is that their every misdemeanour has been well documented over the years for us all to read!

KING EDWARD VIII – THE NAZI LOVING KING
(LATER, DUKE OF WINDSOR)
b.1894 d.1972
Reigned during 1936

King George V died on 20 January 1936 and the Prince of Wales was proclaimed as King Edward VIII on 21 and 22 January. He flew from Sandringham to London (the first British monarch to travel by air). George V's funeral took place on 28 January. Edward VIII was a colourful and modern character, well travelled and a good communicator. However, he had a poor understanding of the working relationship between monarch and ministers. He had an even worse understanding of foreign affairs, which was seen in his adulation of Hitler.

It was Edward's relationship which an American divorcee that caused a constitutional crisis. He met Wallis Simpson at a party in 1931. The government of the day rejected the relationship which gathered pace over the next five years. Prime Minister Stanley Baldwin warned Edward that the British people would not accept an American as their Queen. Edward proposed a morganatic marriage, where the King's partner is a consort rather than a queen. The Cabinet rejected the idea.

King Edward VIII's reign ended on 11 December. His reign had lasted just three hundred and twenty-five days. It was, in fact, the shortest reign of any recognised monarch since King Edward V. Other historians mention Lady Jane Grey, Edgar the Atheling and Sweyn Forkbeard. In November 1936, he made his famous radio speech to the nation via the BBC, explaining his reasons for abdication, with the immortal words . . .

'I have found it impossible to carry the heavy burden of responsibility and to discharge my duties as King, as I would wish to do, without the help and support of the woman I love.'

His brother became King George VI and Edward married Wallis Simpson in France, in June 1937. During the Second World War he was moved to the Bahamas and was made Governor. This whole episode was, of course, a scandal in itself. But the other big scandal of King Edward VIII and Wallis Simpson, or the Duke and Duchess of Windsor as they were later known, were their pro-Nazi views, which they made no effort in hiding from the British people.

King Edward VIII

No End in Sight!

In October 1937, the Duke and Duchess of Windsor visited Germany and met Adolf Hitler. This was against the advice of the British Government. His visit, including his Nazi salute was all over the German press. Hitler and his senior officials said the relationship between Britain and Germany could have been different if Edward had still been King. Edward had made no secret of the fact he wanted to personally visit Hitler. When he was advised against it by Prime Minister Stanley Baldwin, a German envoy pointed this out to him. However, Edward asked, 'Who is King here, Baldwin or I?' and demanded his request be passed on to the Fuhrer. This direct communication broke all constitutional protocol. In 1939, at the outbreak of war, the Duke and Duchess of Windsor lived in France. When Germany invaded, they fled south, and later to Portugal. The German Minister in The Hague at the time accused the couple of leaking Allied war plans for the defence of Belgium. In another sign of Edward's special relationship with the Nazis, he apparently asked for German guards to be put outside his homes in Paris and on the Riviera, which they did. There are stories of Edward blubbing sensitive British information to the wrong people at the wrong functions. Some argue his tongue compromised the safety of his own country. At one point Winston Churchill threatened Edward with a court martial unless he returned to Britain. Instead the couple were taken to the Bahamas.

In 1940, a well-known American journalist Fulton Oursler was summoned by Edward, as Governor of the Bahamas. Oursler reported that Edward gave him a eulogy to Hitler, calling him a great man and stating it would be a terrible thing if he were to be defeated. Edward told the journalist to ask President Roosevelt to offer to intervene and mediate for peace in Europe. FBI documents later claimed that the British Government wouldn't back the marriage of Edward and Wallis because they already knew that she had pro-Nazi views. Wallis had even been accused of sleeping with the German Ambassador to London. This begs the question: was Edward prevented from marrying because of constitutional matters, or because of his and her Nazi views? The abdication was, of course, at a time when the Nazi regime was limbering up in Europe, acting in an aggressive and threatening manner. Edward's suitability as a future king was probably in question. Was the Mrs Simpson scandal convenient fodder to get rid of the Reich-loving royal?

The royal family had been trying to shake off its German heritage for years, even changing their name to Windsor. Some may have seen Edward as almost half-German. He spoke fluent German and was descended from the Hanoverian King George I, and more recently his great-grandfather Prince Albert. In *Royal Scandals* Nigel Cawthorne says there are several possible reasons why Edward was forced to abdicate rather than being allowed to marry Wallis Simpson. He suggests some had a problem with Simpson's nationality (American), others because of her social standing (commoner), some because she was a divorcee (twice), but acknowledges the suggestion that the crisis was an excuse to get rid of the pro-fascist royal. Some say this latter reason is just too far-fetched, but can it really be ruled out? Baldwin's cabinet was not impressed with Edward's pro-Nazi rhetoric.

It's believed by some historians that Hitler planned to put Edward back on the throne in a new Nazi Britain. Edward was regarded with great suspicion. In 1941, when he and Wallis Simpson visited Florida, US President Franklin D. Roosevelt had the pair put under secret surveillance. There were unconfirmed reports that Wallis Simpson had stayed in contact with the German Ambassador in London. There was a worry she had been leaking intelligence as well.

There are also claims that MI5 was sent to Germany at the end of the war to take back private and sensitive letters between Edward and Adolf Hitler. Some of those letters were apparently lost or stolen; make of that what you want! Meanwhile, in Edward's memoirs he denied ever being pro-Nazi and made fun of Hitler. However, he did admit that he admired the German nation. He died in 1972, in France. Queen Elizabeth visited him on his death bed. Edward was given a full royal funeral.

The late Queen Mother hated Wallis, calling her Mrs S, rather than by her official title of the Duchess of Windsor. In a private letter published in a biography about her (2009), it says she did not speak to Wallis Simpson after the abdication in 1936, for 36 years, right up until the Duke's funeral in 1972. In fact, Edward and Wallis had been banned from coming to Britain without the consent of the royal family. They had threatened to cut off his allowance if he disobeyed the order.

H. Matthew says in *ODNB*, the Duke of Windsor, behaved with dignity and reserve after the abdication. He says the Duke and his wife saw it as a deliberate and systematic exclusion. Many thought Edward was calling everyone's bluff when he said he could not be King without Wallis, but he meant it. Matthew, at least, pays tribute to that characteristic, saying there have been few better examples of fidelity in a person.

Old, frail, and senile, the Duchess died 14 years later. She was buried alongside her husband, as 'Wallis, Duchess of Windsor'.

EDWARD'S ABDICATION SPEECH

'At long last I am able to say a few words of my own. I have never wanted to withhold anything, but until now it has not been constitutionally possible for me to speak.

A few hours ago I discharged my last duty as King and Emperor, and now that I have been succeeded by my brother, the Duke of York, my first words must be to declare my allegiance to him. This I do with all my heart.

You all know the reasons which have impelled me to renounce the throne. But I want you to understand that in making up my mind I did not forget the country or the empire, which, as Prince of Wales and lately as King, I have for 25 years tried to serve.

But you must believe me when I tell you that I have found it impossible to carry the heavy burden of responsibility and to discharge my duties as King as I would wish to do without the help and support of the woman I love.

And I want you to know that the decision I have made has been mine and mine alone. This was a thing I had to judge entirely for myself. The other person most nearly concerned has tried up to the last to persuade me to take a different course.

I have made this, the most serious decision of my life, only upon the single thought of what would, in the end, be best for all. This decision has been made less difficult to me by the sure knowledge that my brother, with his long training in the public affairs of this country and with his fine qualities, will be able to take my place forthwith without interruption or injury to the life and progress of the empire. And he has one matchless blessing, enjoyed by so many of you, and not bestowed on me – a happy home with his wife and children.

During these hard days I have been comforted by her majesty, my mother, and by my family. The ministers of the Crown, and in particular, Mr Baldwin, the Prime Minister, have always treated me with full consideration. There has never been any constitutional difference between me and them, and between me and Parliament. Bred in the constitutional tradition by my father, I should never have allowed any such issue to arise.

Ever since I was Prince of Wales, and later on when I occupied the throne, I have been treated with the greatest kindness by all classes of the people wherever I have lived or journeyed throughout the empire. For that I am very grateful.

I now quit altogether public affairs and I lay down my burden. It may be some time before I return to my native land, but I shall always follow the fortunes of the British race and empire with profound interest, and if at any time in the future I can be found of service to his majesty in a private station, I shall not fail.

And now, we all have a new King. I wish him and you, his people, happiness and prosperity with all my heart. God bless you all! God save the King!'

Just when the current Royals could be forgiven for thinking that the Nazi connection was all over, one of the younger Royal Princes stuck his foot in it!

HARRY DRESSES AS A NAZI

This was a story that was on the front page of the *Sun* newspaper in January 2005. A thoughtless Prince Harry, third in line to the throne, decided to dress up as a Nazi soldier at a fancy dress party. A photograph of him in a Nazi desert uniform with a swastika armband clearly on show, drinking, with a cigarette in hand and a big grin on his face, was flashed around the world. Prince William had had enough sense to dress in something a little more conservative; a lion outfit. On Harry's choice of costume there was condemnation from politicians and Jewish organisations everywhere. Clarence House issued an immediate apology, and Harry, aged 20 at the time, made his own apology too:

'I am very sorry if I caused any offence or embarrassment to anyone. It was a poor choice of costume and I apologise'.

After the incident some prominent figures questioned the Prince's suitability to attend the royal military college at Sandhurst, where he was due to start later that year. Former Armed Forces Minister, Doug

Henderson MP, said the Prince should no longer to be allowed to become an officer of the British army and his application for the Academy should be withdrawn. However, the Ministry of Defence said his behaviour at a private party would not affect his application. The picture was taken at a friend's birthday party in Wiltshire where the fancy dress theme had been 'colonial and native'.

If Harry had dressed at a Nazi at any other time, it would still have been a disgrace and caused outrage. But you can imagine the whole of the Royal Family holding their head-in-hands at the cringe-worthy timing of the incident. It was coming up to the Holocaust Memorial Day, the 60th anniversary of the liberation of Auschwitz, a royal visit to the death camp and a reception for death camp survivors to be held by the Queen at St James's Palace. The incident also brought back embarrassing and unpleasant memories for the Royals and their links to the murderous Nazi regime for, as we have just seen, King Edward VIII was a Nazi sympathiser. (See page 96.)

THE DUKE OF HAZARD, PRINCE PHILIP AND HIS BIG MOUTH
b. 1921

The Duke of Hazard is the nickname often given to blunder-mouth Prince Philip, the Duke of Edinburgh. He is known for opening his mouth before putting his brain into gear. He has come out with so many gaffes and errors of judgement, there does not seem to be a section of society he has not upset or offended in some way. Is he just being ironic? Perhaps un-PC because of his age, maybe he is a loveable old rogue who slips up from time to time, or maybe he is an out-of-touch, rude, over-privileged, on-a-different-planet, royal. On the other hand he has served his country well. He is the longest serving consort in the history of the monarchy. He is in charge of the Duke of Edinburgh Award Scheme. He is the husband of Queen Elizabeth II and was made a Prince of the United Kingdom in 1957. He has spoken widely on his passion, the relationship between the environment and humanity. He has always supported science, sport and education and has made many goodwill trips around the globe.

SOME OF PHILIP'S MOST NOTORIOUS GAFFES

1955   He decided to blunder in and comment on the stress counselling offered to servicemen and women, and moaned, 'We didn't have counsellors rushing around every time somebody let off a gun, asking, are you all right? Are you sure you don't have a ghastly problem?'

1966 He upset a lot of women in Britain saying, 'British women can't cook,' a sweeping statement that upset many people.

1969 At a Royal Variety performance he once asked singer Tom Jones if he gargled with pebbles.

1969 He also described Adam Faith's voice as sounding like bath water going down the plug hole.

1981 During this time there was massive unemployment in Britain but the Prince showed his insensitive side yet again by announcing, 'Everybody was saying we must have more leisure. Now they are complaining they are unemployed.'

1984 As a woman took great delight in giving a small gift to the Prince during his visit to Kenya, he asked her, 'You are a woman, aren't you?'

1986 During a state visit to China in 1986, he warned a small group of British students, 'If you stay here much longer, you'll all be slitty-eyed.'

Big Mouth, Duke of Edinburgh

1986   He told a World Wildlife Fund meeting, 'If it has got four legs and it is not a chair, if it has got two wings and it flies but is not an aeroplane, and if it swims and it is not a submarine, the Cantonese will eat it,' promptly upsetting an entire race.

1991   After accepting a conservation award abroad he told the audience, 'Your country is one of the most notorious centres of trading in endangered species in the world.'

1993   When he met a British student in Budapest, Philip went about upsetting many Hungarians by telling him, 'You can't have been here that long – you haven't got a pot belly.'

1994   A visit to the Cayman Islands saw Prince Philip famously sticking his foot in it yet again, asking an islander, 'Aren't most of you descended from pirates?'

1995   He asked a driving instructor in Oban, Scotland, 'How do you keep the natives off the booze long enough to get them through the test?'

1995   During calls to ban the gun after the Dunblane school shooting Prince Philip chipped in with, 'If a cricketer, for instance, suddenly decided to go into a school and batter a lot of people to death with a cricket bat, which he could do very easily, I mean, are you going to ban cricket bats?'

1996   During a conversation with a matron of a hospital in the Caribbean, he told the matron, 'You have mosquitoes. I have the press.' (Quoted in Andrew Duncan's, *The Reality of Monarchy*)

1997   'Bloody silly fool!' A Cambridge University car park attendant did not recognise Philip and got this arrogant response.

1998   He told a student who had been trekking through Papua New Guinea, 'You managed not to get eaten, then?'

1999   When he saw an old and dubious looking fuse box hanging on a wall at a factory near Edinburgh, the Prince blurted out the classic, but completely un-politically correct line, 'It looks as if it was put in by an Indian.'

1999   When visiting a man in Lockerbie who had lost 11 neighbours when the plane came down, what words of comfort did Philip offer the man? Try this . . . 'People usually say that after a fire it is water damage that is the worst. We are still trying to dry out Windsor Castle.'

1999   When visiting a deaf school he commented on a rather loud steel band and said 'Deaf? If you are near there, no wonder you are deaf.'

2001   When a 13-year-old boy excitedly told the Prince, during a visit to the University of Salford, that he was desperate to be astronaut when he grew up, the Prince did not offer much in the way of support. His response was to tell the boy he (the boy) needed to lose weight if he was going to fit into a spaceship.

2002   He ignorantly asked an Australian Aborigine if he was still throwing spears around.

2002   He upset a woman in a wheel chair who had her guide dog with her, by telling her, 'Do you know they are producing eating dogs for anorexics now?'

2002   The Prince met a teenage Army cadet who had lost some of his sight after picking up a disguised Real IRA bomb in West London. The Queen made polite and concerned conversation with the brave teenager, and asked Stephen Menary how much of his sight was still left. The gaffe-prone Prince, looking at the boy's loud and colourful tie, interrupted and said, 'Not a lot, judging by that tie.' The lad's mother was present and said the Queen looked annoyed at the Prince. Stephen's mother said she did not think Philip meant to offend them, but was just joking to break the ice. Stephen, now grown up, recalls how he got his own back a year after the incident. He was on parade at the Jubilee celebrations going past Buckingham Palace and flashed his giant union jack tie at Philip, as if to say, 'This one's even worse!'

2006   When a young man was telling Philip he was going to Romania to work with orphans, Philip said he thought the Romanians were breeding children just to put them in orphanages, because there was so many of them around.

2009   At a reception to celebrate the country's most successful Asian business people, he looked at one man's name tag, which had Patel written on it and told the man, 'There's a lot of your family here tonight.'

2009   He even asked President Obama if he could tell the difference between all the foreign leaders.

PRINCE EDWARD, JUST LIKE HIS FATHER!
b. 1964 –

It is not only Prince Philip who makes such royal gaffes. It would seem that Prince Edward has inherited his father's ability to open his mouth before putting his brain into gear too, for it was he who caused upset and outrage during a visit to mark the 50th anniversary of the Duke of Edinburgh Award scheme, in Sydney in October 2009. He rather stupidly suggested, in a newspaper interview, that the death of a boy taking part in an outdoor pursuit, as part of the scheme back in 1961, could have attracted more participants. Edward said the death of the boy, called Ray, boosted the scheme's popularity. He said, 'Suddenly the award, which was new . . . its reputation among young people was, "Wow, this is serious. You could die doing this."' Ray's brother Ken said he was absolutely horrified that the Prince could say something so stupid and insensitive, and that it brought back all those hurt feelings. It was supposed to be a low-key visit, but Edward's crass remarks ruined that plan.

Ray and more than 20 other teenagers and young people had been taking part in an outdoor training exercise, to get their achievement medal from the award. But three of the team, including Ray, disappeared. Police scoured the countryside for them. One of the boys stumbled back to base camp a day later, suffering from exposure and exhaustion. The other was found unconscious, but survived. Ray never made it. The weather conditions were tough, and Ray died of exposure, alone and outside. Ken eventually got his medal at Buckingham Palace, and the Duke of Edinburgh himself took Ken's family into a private room to express his condolences to them.

To make matters worse Prince Edward said he did not even know about 17 year old David Iredale, who died of dehydration after getting lost in the Bush in 2006, also as part of the award scheme. He made his insensitive comments about Ray, after being asked about David.

THE LOVE LIFE OF DIANA, PRINCESS OF WALES
b.1961 d.1997

Beatrix Campbell's *Diana Princess of Wales, How Sexual Politics Shook the Monarchy* says Diana was the most seen woman in the world, and never has a young woman been so publicly sexualised. Her public marriage split, and allegation that there were three of them in it (reference to Camilla), scandalised the monarchy and scandalised her own life. Some would argue Diana did not help herself, with rumours of 'special relationships' taking up so many column inches in the tabloids. She may not have perpetuated the rumour machine, but she certainly didn't slow it down. Let us not forget, no matter how popular she was, and how nice she was, there were a number of men labelled as 'close to her'. How close we will never know, although she was obviously very close to her last partner Dodi Fayed. Other men linked to Diana included: James Gilbey, James Hewitt, Will Carling and Doctor Hasnat Khan. To allow herself to be linked to all these men was perhaps, un-queenly behaviour. If any of the rumours of being romantically linked to other men was untrue, the Palace press team or her press advisors should have worked harder to dispel them. But this is where royal press departments often fail. Royal press officers can be very guarded at times. They should be carriers of information, not guard dogs of scandal.

SQUIDGYGATE

British Intelligence was supposed to be keeping an eye on Diana, the Princess of Wales, after details of her mental health appeared in Andrew Morton's biography about her. Several stories had been circulating about alleged inflicting of self-harm, bulimia and claims about Charles's relationship with Camilla. Intelligence had centred on her special friendship with a man called James Gilbey. There is no definitive proof, but tapes came out of the two of them supposedly having a private conversation. The newspapers dubbed the incident 'SquidgyGate'. Some experts claimed Diana's phone line at Sandringham had a bug placed on it. During the taped calls, the man supposed to be Gilbey, called Diana and talked about her worries about getting pregnant. It's thought the conversation had actually taken place in 1989. Two members of the public said they had made the recordings whilst listening in to wireless broadcasts. Others remain convinced that the recordings were actually a lot more sinister, i.e. professionally made. As pre-divorce discussions commenced, there was a battle between Charles and Diana for public sympathy at the time. *The Sun* newspaper ran its own copy of the tape. Readers could call a premium rate phone line and listen in to the conversation. However, parts of the tape had been edited out and withheld from readers. Extra copies of the conversation had also been given to another newspaper and a magazine as well. The question remained, was Diana's phone bugged? Diana herself thought that was the case. Morton's speculation on the alleged recording of the private conversation was included in his 1993 book. He asked whether it was some kind of bluff, or whether it was actually true. The then Home Secretary, Kenneth Clarke, announced that there was absolutely no evidence to suggest Diana's phone had been bugged, as she had suspected. In 1993, Diana retired from public life, and a year later Charles admitted on television that he had been unfaithful. Not long after that, the memoirs of a soldier called James Hewitt claimed he had had an affair with Diana as early as 1986. But the revelations were bad timing and public opinion turned against Hewitt, calling him indiscreet, and he fled to France.

DEATH OF DIANA

But one could argue the real scandal surrounding the Princess of Wales was the constant paparazzi attention. She was hounded by snooping photographers. She died in that car crash, trying to escape the paparazzi. Or is the scandal that you and I paid money for newspapers that had photos of Diana and Dodi on 'that' holiday. We, as a nation, had hounded her out of the country. On Mohamed Al Fayed's official website, where he tells the story of her love affair with his son Dodi, he says she did not want to live in the UK permanently anymore because of media harassment. Ironically, she thought she would be safer from prying press lenses in Paris. Her relationship with Dodi Al Fayed was just about to be made more special and more permanent. Just before they died, he had bought her an engagement ring and they were on the way back to his apartment where he was going to ask her to marry him. They never made it there. Both were killed after their car crashed.

Further scandal surrounded Diana, even after her death. Mohamed Al Fayed was so upset over his son's death he wanted answers. He immediately accused rogue British intelligence workers of bumping off the couple. There are plenty of conspiracy theories, from faked death, to assassination. One conspiracy website says Diana told the *Daily Mail* just before the crash she was going to withdraw from public life. Meanwhile, on Mohamed Al Fayed's website, he says Dodi had bought them a place in Malibu, so they would be far away from public life in the UK.

It is these claims of renegade MI6 agents arranging Diana's death that created the biggest scandal surrounding the monarchy for generations. There is supposed to be an anonymous note hidden away at Scotland Yard, naming two secret agents linked to Diana's death. Nobody knows their identity. The note claims to be from the CIA. It could have been some crackpot of course. There have been many questions asked about the driver of the Mercedes that night, Henri Paul, who had lots of money put into his bank, leading up to the crash. He is dead, so he cannot tell us anything. But one of his close friends told the press that the memory of his friend was being tarnished as a way of hiding something that both the British and French establishments wanted to hide.

Coroner Lord Justice Scott Baker opened the inquest at the High Court in London, in October 2007. The jury, of six men and five women, heard how Diana had previously feared being killed off in a car accident, perhaps from brake failure. The judge told the jury there had been much speculation about the crash in the Pont de l'Alma tunnel, in Paris. He reiterated Mohamed Al Fayed's claims that MI6 had been commissioned to compile a report on his family for the Royal Family. Sir Richard Dearlove gave evidence at the inquest into the deaths of Diana and Dodi Fayed to rebut claims made by Mohamed al Fayed that Diana and his son Dodi were killed by MI6 on the orders of the Duke of Edinburgh. Michael Mansfield QC was acting for Mohamed al Fayed and questioned Sir Richard. At the 2008 hearing, he denied either Diana or Dodi Fayed were of any interest to the service in any way. Dearlove was MI6's Director of Operations from 1994 to 1999. He denied that any assassinations took place under his authority and took the allegations as 'personal.'

In April 2008, the coroner threw out the case, telling the jury that there was no evidence to support claims by Mohamed Al Fayed that the couple were killed in an establishment plot. Two-hundred and fifty witnesses later, Lord Justice Scott Baker said there was no evidence to support the allegations. The coroner told the jury it could not rule in favour of Mohamed Al Fayed's allegations of unlawful killing, but they could rule in favour of unlawful killing by the gross negligence of driver Henri Paul. The jury therefore ruled Diana and Dodi were unlawfully killed due to the actions of their driver, who was over the limit, and the actions of the paparazzi. Since the acci-dent in 1997, British and French investigations have also ruled it was an accident.

SARAH, THE DUCHESS OF YORK, AND THAT TOE-SUCKING INCIDENT
b.1959

The Duchess is the daughter of the late Major Ronald Ferguson and the late Susan Barrantes. She met Prince Andrew at a party in 1985, and they married in 1986. They have two daughters; Princess Beatrice, born in 1988, and Princess Eugenie born in 1990. By 1992, the couple had drifted apart. Sarah blamed it on Andrew being away at sea on naval duties. She gave a revealing More4 TV interview to Pamela Stephenson in which she claimed she was not supported by Buckingham Palace when her husband was abroad on duty. She said Prince Andrew was only home for 40 days a year in the first five years of their marriage. Sarah and Prince Andrew agreed to separate in January 1992. Seven months later one of the most scandalous photographs ever connected to the royals, was printed; it appeared in *The Daily Mirror*. The Duchess was topless and was having her toes sucked by the financial advisor John Bryan, at an exclusive resort in the south of France. The toe-sucking photos appeared everywhere, worldwide. The royals were open to massive ridicule. The paparazzi had made an overnight financial killing. The Angeli Agency in Paris, which took the infamous photo, said it had made enough money from that one picture alone, to buy a very nice three bedroom house in Paris. It brought into question the behaviour of the younger royals. The Duchess's bare breasts were splashed across the world. The royal family was dragged through the gutter. The former daughter-in-law to the Queen was brandishing her nipples across every breakfast table in the world. The photos may have been surreptitiously taken, but the damage had been done. Sarah was no longer a royal, technically, but it made no difference. She was Prince Andrew's wife (albeit on paper) seen in the company of a number of men, Bryan and also the Texan multi-millionaire Steve Wyatt.

By the time of their divorce in 1996, Sarah was reportedly in debt to the tune of more than four million pounds. She was overweight and had earned herself the nickname the Duchess of Pork. She retreated to the US where she felt she was far enough removed from the royal family to start working commercially. Her jobs included:

- Weight Watchers spokesperson (after losing the weight)
- Charity campaigner
- Chat show host (sitting in for Larry King)

- Writer and producer
- Author of *Budgie the Helicopter* books and TV shows
- Spokesperson for several companies
- After dinner public speaker
- Modelling: She posed for *Harper's Bazaar* brandishing a riding crop and wearing high heels shoes and fishnets! (Shockingly, nobody called that a scandal!)
- She also modelled for *Vogue*

One of the more recent scandals to hit the Yorks is the cost of their daughters' police protection, which is reportedly around £250,000 per year. Whilst hard-working Brits are handing over their cash for their police protection, the young Princesses have become the paparazzi's dream. They are often snapped at premiers and parties and in 2008, on her gap year, Beatrice was seen enjoying her break in the Caribbean.

FIVE LITTLE MODERN-DAY ROYAL SCANDALS

Some scandals are so immense and so shocking that they have the potential to rock the very core of the Monarchy: others are merely disturbing, especially for those who have placed members of royal families on a pedestal.

NOT THE PERFECT WEDDING PHOTOS

In 1999 Sophie Rhys-Jones became engaged to Prince Edward. After the wedding she became known as the Countess of Wessex. But Sophie was involved in an unfortunate scandal just before her wedding day.

How the story was treated was more of a scandal than anything else. Sophie Rhys-Jones, as she was known before her wedding, used to work for Capital Radio in London, a few years before I worked there. On a working trip, a colleague apparently pulled up her top in a playful manner, and someone took a photo of her. She can be seen laughing at the horse play. Now, it all seemed like a bit of fun, although it may not be the idea of fun to everyone. It was Sophie's own private business, until she was getting married to the Queen's youngest son. A DJ at the radio station, who had by then moved else-where, sold the pictures to the *Sun* newspaper for a reported £100,000. They were immediately printed. It was just before Sophie's wedding day. The nation was outraged. *The Sun* had misjudged the nation and was left red-faced. Nobody wants to upset a bride just before her big day. *The Sun*, in all fairness, issued a grovelling apology to Sophie on its pages. It was criticised by its readers, its competitors, politicians and the palace. The story went worldwide instantly. The *Daily News* in New York, for instance, reported that the Queen was horrified and had made a complaint to the Press Complaints Commission, calling the publishing of the photos, cruel. The wedding went ahead in June 1999 at Windsor Castle. Edward and Sophie apparently decided they wanted to have a low key ceremony.

THE PORN STAR AND THE PRINCE

Dashingly handsome Prince Andrew, or Randy Andy as the tabloids used to call him, was embroiled in an embarrassing scandal 1981–1983 with his girlfriend Koo Stark. He had been seeing her for about a year and a half, when he was forced to end the romance because it emerged she had once appeared in a soft porn film, called *Emily*. The couple had been enjoying a very close romance, had been followed by the media being photographed in romantic places such as Mustique, and seemed like a seriously romantic couple. But when nude stills from *Emily* appeared in the newspapers, the Prince was forced to end the romance. It was more than the royal family could stomach. The film is a sort of British version of the well-known adult flick *Emmanuelle*, although not quite as rude! It is set in the 1920s, about a girl who returns from her latest term at boarding school to find out her mother, her friends and even the family maid are all having sex with different people, all the time, all over the place. She then decides to lose her virginity and join in the never ending sexual fun. The movie database *imdb.com* says about Koo Stark's film *Emily*, 'Recommended for all the drooling sex fiends out there if no one else.' These days, older, wiser, and a mum herself, Koo has been running her own breast cancer awareness charity, after battling the condition herself.

IT WASN'T THE BUTLER!

A royal butler, a court case, and the Queen herself: a great mix for a royal scandal and a half. When Diana, Princess of Wales, died in 1997, her butler Paul Burrell told the Queen he would hang on to a few of Diana's possessions. On 18 January 2001 Burrell was arrested in a dawn raid on his home in Cheshire. Police searched his house and removed several items. He was charged with stealing many of Diana's possessions. Mr Burrell had worked for the Royal Family for 21 years. He was the Queen's personal footman for a while and Diana personally chose him to work as her butler. The two were very close, and she called him 'her rock'. The Prince of Wales reportedly told some of his friends that he did not want Mr Burrell prosecuted, concerned that William and Harry would be dragged into the police investigation. Items belonging to Diana had been allegedly stolen from Kensington Palace after Diana's death. Paul Burrell denied any wrong doing throughout the investigation. He was eventually taken to court. The Queen initially had trouble remembering Burrell's warning that he had taken the items to look after. There followed an expensive trial. Her Majesty remembered in the nick of time, just days into the trial, at a cost of £1.5m. Following Her Majesty's last minute memory revival, the trial collapsed and Burrell's name was completely cleared; he was an innocent man.

THE ROYAL CRADLE-SNATCHER

Princess Margaret was once amongst the most eligible women in the world. She married the dashing and flamboyant photographer Anthony Armstrong-Jones, later Lord Snowdon. It was the 1960s and they were the young, glamorous, exciting, charming and modern members of the royal family. But their marriage ended in 1978. It was the first royal divorce for more than four hundred years, and it was surrounded in scandal. When they had first met at a party in 1958, Margaret thought Snowdon was not interested in her, or other women for that matter. But Snowdon was 100 per cent straight and had plenty of beautiful girlfriends. They were soon an item, and engaged a year later. They married in 1960. But years later affairs, on both sides, started. Snowdon distanced himself from his wife when she started an affair, and he hooked up with a girl 16 years younger than him.

In 1971 the newspapers were going to reveal all and the Snowdons denied everything. Five years later in a newspaper, pictures appeared of Margaret on holiday on Mustique with a man called Roddy Llewellyn, a landscape gardener 17 years her junior. Finally, an affair that was public. Tony Snowdon left the marriage. The tabloid headlines of the day were quite cruel to Princess Margaret, telling her to dump her lover. They eventually split in 1980 and Margaret was said to be heartbroken. Her marriage though, was well and truly over. She was blamed publicly for the split. The scandal caused shockwaves throughout Britain; a princess playing away.

No End in Sight!

POSSIBLY THE BIGGEST ROYAL SCANDAL OF MODERN TIMES

Well it would be if we actually knew exactly what went on. What we do know is the establishment closed ranks.

An article by Tom Pettifor in *mirror.co.uk* (published 16 Feb 2008), asked if a 1971 bank robbing gang stumbled across rude snaps of Princess Margaret. The gang had tunnelled underground from a shop into the vault of Lloyds Bank on Baker Street, in London, and robbed the contents of a number of safety deposit boxes. It is said that naughty pictures of a naked royal were discovered. It sparked a cover up by police and MI5, and allegations of a royal sex scandal surrounding Princess Margaret. The gang of thieves, nicknamed the sewer rats, tunnelled forty feet underground from a shop, under the floor of Lloyds Bank in London's Baker Street, and straight up into the vault. All they wanted was cash. They got away with half-a-million pounds, more than five million in today's money.

Scandalous items found in the bank's safety deposit boxes.

Details of the heist, the criminals and even their sentences were all hushed up. A government file on them will remain secret until 2054.

The robbers had not bargained for scandalous photos. Supposedly the underworld figure Michael X, a black power leader of the day, had these red-hot photos. But we cannot ask him what was in them because he was executed in 1975. If you can wait until the year 2054 the government file on him will become open to the public. This was at the time of the end of Princess Margaret's marriage to the Earl of Snowdon, and around the time she was seeing a gardener 17 years younger than her. At the time, the press was issued with D-Notices, creating a media black-out.

A film, starring Jason Statham, was made about the story in 2008. The *London Evening Standard* newspaper called it a tale about bank robbers, Soho pornographers, bent policemen, perverse politico and a female royal! One can assume MI5 found the photos, after there were a number of arrests over the robbery. Where the photos are now, what they actually show, and whether they will ever see the light of day again, is all unclear. It is rife for conspiracy theorists to get to work, and for inaccurate or embellished reporting. But for the establishment to hit the panic button and close ranks with such speed, we know the nature of the photos was fairly shocking. Other undesirable photos of people involved in politics, and lists of dubious bribes and payments between other parties were apparently exposed in the robbery. What the robbers saw in full is not clear, whether they will ever speak is also unclear. Frightening, in my opinion, is the power of the government to silence such men, with complete assurances their lips will remain closed forever.

Chapter Six

And Finally Did You Know . . .

Of course a scandal, is a scandal, is a scandal. Not quite because there are so many other factors which go into the mixing pot to make up a scandal – where do those involved live for example, was security tight enough, should there be security, are the privileged more prone to the excesses of life and indeed are some scandals media manufactured? To throw into the controversial, analytical mixing pot there follows some interesting facts.

SECURITY AT BUCKINGHAM PALACE

There have been numerous security incidents at the palace over the years, too many to detail here. However, it's surely a scandal in itself that so many people have got so close to the Royals in recent times. One of the weirdest cases was that of a 12-year-old boy in 1837 who actually managed to live in the palace for a whole YEAR, without being found. He hid in chimneys and dirtied the beds he found to sleep in. He was caught in 1838 and was the subject of a security debate in the House of Commons. Of the seven assassination attempts on Queen Victoria, three of them were within the vicinity of the palace. In theory it is a very secure building, as there are a number of barracks within a few minutes from the gates, soldiers based inside the palace, and its own police station within the walls. There are countless security measures in place that we do not know about. As a young student working at Windsor Castle, I witnessed one or two things that were reassuring, even as a dogsbody, I was given the Official Secrets Act to sign.

Bearing in mind, at the time of writing this, there is a vastly reduced risk of Irish Republican terrorism and a much increased risk from religious extremists one has to ask why it seems as if the security at the palace is insufficient. Security has not improved that much over the years, with suffragettes chaining themselves to the front gates and protesters driving into them too! In 1974 there was an attempted kidnapping of Princess Anne as she drove up to the palace. In 1981 three tourists scaled the garden walls and claimed they thought it was part of Hyde Park. Perhaps the most famous incident was that of Michael Fagan who actually got into the Queen's bedroom as she slept. She managed to keep him calm with polite conversation until help arrived and was praised for her dignified calm response. In 1994 a naked paraglider landed on the roof and in 2004 fathers' rights campaigners also breached security. One dressed as Batman climbed onto the front balcony. The year before an undercover tabloid journalist got a job as a palace footman using one fake and one real reference, and managed to take photos of the Queen's breakfast room, the Duke of York's bedroom, and the bedroom where the US President George W. Bush was about to stay on his state visit. The reporter worked there for two months. Once again, the scandal of the lack of security was discussed in the House of Commons. The newspapers described the reference checking as 'scandalous'. The palace took action against the newspaper for an invasion of privacy.

Security at the palace should be almost fail-safe, and the number of breaches over the years has proved that those responsible for the safety need to improve their game. I am not privy to any inside information, and I am sure there have been many incidents cleverly thwarted by the hard work and dedication of security personnel, but just one or two serious incidents is a worry.

ROYAL RESIDENCES

We may have only one home – and a holiday home perhaps, if we are very lucky – but the Royals have numerous residences which surely can only compound their problems. For example they have to worry whether the lights are out and the iron is unplugged (well maybe not them exactly!) in numerous Royal residences, such as:

- Balmoral Castle
- Buckingham Palace
- Clarence House
- Frogmore
- Kensington Palace
- Palace of Holyroodhouse
- Queen's Gallery (The), Buckingham Palace
- Queen's Gallery (The), Palace of Holyroodhouse
- Royal Mews (The), Buckingham Palace

- Sandringham House
- St James's Palace
- Windsor Castle

ROYAL BUILDINGS

It doesn't end there either for the following buildings have strong royal connections. They have all been bases or places of temporary/permanent residence for certain members of the royal family. Some have been owned by Royals others were or are now in private hands. This guide is for basic information only. All of these properties, their full histories and availability to the public are detailed on their own particular websites.

St James's Palace. A busy office and home of past and present royals and staff, commissioned by Henry VIII, and built on the site of an old hospital.

ALLERTON CASTLE, NORTH YORKSHIRE
Supposedly once the home of Prince Frederick Augustus who was the real life 'Grand Old Duke of York', immortalised in the nursery rhyme of the same name.

AUDLEY END HOUSE, SAFFRON WALDEN, ESSEX
Henry VIII gave abbey lands to Sir Thomas Audley, who converted the abbey buildings to use as his own mansion. The house and extensive gardens are now carefully looked after by English Heritage. It was later given to the Suffolk family.

THE BANQUETING HOUSE
This is the only remaining part of Whitehall Palace, and is well known as the site where King Charles I was executed. Still attracting visitors, it was designed in 1619.

PALACE OF BEAULIEU, CHELMSFORD, ESSEX
This building is steeped in history. New Hall was sold by Thomas Boleyn to Henry VIII in 1517 who rebuilt the house in brick; Queen Elizabeth I then gave it to Thomas Radcliffe, third Earl of Sussex. In 1798 the building was purchased by nuns who changed it into a school. It is still a school today!

CAMBRIDGE COTTAGE, KEW
Set in three hundred acres of grounds, Cambridge Cottage, was home to King George III. It is now available to hire out for weddings.

CARISBROOKE CASTLE, NEWPORT, ISLE OF WIGHT
Edward I bought this building in 1293 but it was not a royal residence until Charles I was held there for more than a year, before his execution. It was also the home of Princess Beatrice, daughter of Queen Victoria. It is now looked after by English Heritage.

CHRIST CHURCH, OXFORD
Not everyone realises that King Charles I lived in the Deanery and held his Parliament in the Great Hall during the Civil War.

CLAREMONT, ESHER, SURREY
In 1816 Claremont was bought by the nation as a wedding present for George IV's daughter Princess Charlotte and her husband Prince

Leopold of Saxe-Coburg. Princess Charlotte died there after giving birth to a stillborn son the following year.

CLAREMONT

Queen Victoria bought this property for her youngest son Leopold, Duke of Albany. It is now looked after by the National Trust. The British Government confiscated it from Leopold's son in 1922, because they hated the fact he had served in the German Army in the First World War.

DUNFERMLINE PALACE, DUNFERMLINE

Dunfermline Palace was rebuilt by King James IV in 1500. It was a favourite residence of a number of Scottish monarchs. King James IV, King James V, Mary Queen of Scots and King James VI all frequented it.

EDINBURGH CASTLE, EDINBURGH

This is one of the oldest royal buildings. It was built in the Ninth Century and has served as a royal palace, a treasury and a prison too. It was also a barracks until 1923. Edinburgh Castle is now looked after by Historic Scotland.

ELTHAM PALACE, KENT

This was used as a royal residence from the Fourteenth to the Sixteenth Century. The original building was given to Edward II in 1305 as a gift from the Bishop of Durham. English Heritage took control of it in 1995.

HAMPTON COURT PALACE

Hampton Court Palace is best known as the home of King Henry VIII and was originally built by Thomas Wolsey, then Archbishop of York and Chief Minister to the King, in 1514. The residence of William III and Mary, it underwent major alterations and improvements to the gardens 300 years ago.

HATFIELD HOUSE, HERTFORDSHIRE

The earlier royal palace on the site dates back to 1485. Just a small part of it still remains today though. The young Princess Elizabeth (later Elizabeth I) lived here, and visitors can see the spot where she was told she had become Queen. Lands around the house and the

Old Palace were owned by King Henry VIII. His children, Elizabeth, Edward and Mary all lived in the Old Palace for a time. The newer house is privately owned.

KEW PALACE
Queen Charlotte lived here, as did King George III when his health was failing.

LEEDS CASTLE, KENT
Over a century and a half it was held by six queens as a dower payment. They include: Eleanor of Castile, Margaret of France, Isabella of France, Joan of Navarre, Anne of Bohemia and Catherine de Valois. King Henry VIII visited the castle many times with Catherine of Aragon. It is now in private hands.

THE CASTLE OF MEY, NEAR JOHN O' GROATS
This was built by George, Earl of Caithness. The Queen Mother bought it in 1952. The castle's upkeep is funded by The Queen Elizabeth Castle of Mey Trust. It opens to the public every summer.

OATLANDS PALACE, WEYBRIDGE, SURREY
Oatlands Palace was a main Royal Palace situated between Weybridge and Walton on Thames, in Surrey, frequented by Henry VIII. Today, a modern housing estate and a hotel sit on the site.

OSBORNE HOUSE, ISLE OF WIGHT
Queen Victoria lived here (1846–1901), after she bought it from Lady Isabella Blachford in 1845. King Edward VII gave the house and most of the estate to the nation in 1902, when he was having a huge clear out of his mother's (Queen Victoria) belongings. It is now run by English Heritage.

QUEEN'S HOUSE, GREENWICH
This was originally part of the Royal Palace of Greenwich. Building started in 1616.

ROYAL PAVILION, BRIGHTON (THE)
This was the marine residence of King George IV as Prince of Wales, Regent and King. It was built in the early 1800s. Queen Victoria

stayed here a little, but apparently did not like it too much. Her last visit was in 1845. It is now owned and managed by the town.

SOMERSET HOUSE, LONDON
The original building dates from the mid 1500s. It is situated between the Strand and the Thames in central London. It was occupied by Edward Seymour, Lord Protector to Edward VI. It later became a naval office, then a public records office, and recently a cultural centre.

STIRLING CASTLE, STIRLINGSHIRE
In King James IV's reign (1488–1513), he spent a lot of money making the castle fit for a monarch, improving it as much as he could. Mary Queen of Scots was crowned there in 1543, and her son, the future James VI, was baptised there in 1566.

TOWER OF LONDON (THE)
The Tower of London was founded in 1078 by William the Conqueror who ordered the White Tower to be built inside the city walls. It has since been used as a prison, execution place, palace and even a zoo. It now houses the Crown Jewels.

PALACE OF WESTMINSTER, LONDON
This palace sits between the River Thames and Westminster Abbey. The original Palace of Westminster was created as a residence for Edward the Confessor. It stayed as the main residence of the Sovereign until 1512. At this point King Henry VIII moved to Whitehall Palace. The site is now known as the Houses of Parliament. Some of the old foundations are still intact.

MURDERED MONARCHS
The definition of the word regicide is the deliberate killing of a monarch. In British tradition, if a king or queen regnant is tried and executed, it still counts as regicide. Regicide therefore includes Mary Queen of Scots and Charles I of England. Other monarchs have been murdered in a less formal way, struck down by a sword, or attacked by captors, enemies, family or friends.

THIS LIST IS A SAMPLE OF 'MURDERED' MONARCHS, AND IS BY NO MEANS EXHAUSTIVE

William II: Killed by an arrow in the New Forest. Unclear if it was an accident or murder

John: Suspected of being poisoned

Edward II: Murdered in prison by his guards who thrust a red hot poker into his anus

Richard II: Died in prison. Unclear how, but thought to have been murdered

Nicholas II of Russia: Executed by his captors in 1918

Edward V: One of the Princes in the Tower, possibly smothered to death

Peter III of Russia 1728–1762: Was supposedly assassinated because of a conspiracy led by his wife. She then succeeded him to the throne as Catherine II

Of course as far as the British Royal family are concerned all of this could have been so different, and some of these scandalous incidents would be rather uninteresting if the following scandal could be substantiated.

KING MICHAEL I, MICHAEL ABNEY-HASTINGS, FARMER OR KING OF ENGLAND?
1942 -

Whose crown is it anyway?

It is impossible to discuss royal scandals without mentioning research highlighted by a Channel 4 documentary screened in 2004 *Britain's Real Monarch*, which asked if Queen Elizabeth II is the rightful Queen, or has the real royal family lost out on its true inheritance. The programme, presented by Tony Robinson, examined evidence that suggested King Edward IV, (reigned 1461–1483 with a short gap), was in fact illegitimate. ABC Television described it as rewriting five hundred years of history. The programme accused King Edward IV of being born out of wedlock. This would not only cancel his right to the throne, but all of his descendants since, including Queen Elizabeth II.

It's a genealogical nightmare examining the full family tree, but suffice to say the findings are based on Edward IV's mother Lady Cecily Neville supposedly having an affair with an archer named Blaybourne when her husband, Richard, Duke of York was away in battle in France. He was, in fact, several days march away at the supposed time of conception. Some researchers claim Cecily confessed in a rage many years later, claiming her son was a 'bastard'. Therefore Cecily's and Richard's legitimate son George, Duke of Clarence, should have been the real heir and his descendants thereafter.

Other research claims there was illegitimacy through Edward IV's maternal line, stating his mother Cecily was descended from Edward III and Henry II, a line tainted by the union of John of Gaunt and Katherine. At this point, I must point out that most historians have rejected this research, despite documents suggesting Edward IV's supposed father was away for a five-week period. To make this 'story' or 'research' (whatever your view) even more fascinating, there is another scandalous twist. Descendants of one of Richard's and Cecily's real heirs survive today. The TV programme, which was shown in the US and Australia as well, tracked down the end of the genealogical line, in other words, the man who should by birthright now be King of England, if it had continued to exist as a separate kingdom to Scotland. Michael Abney-Hastings, the fourteenth Earl of Loudoun, is a direct descendant of Cecily's son George, Duke of Clarence, on the Plantagenet line. He was tracked down and presented with the evidence. The 'real' King of England apparently finds the research amusing but has no intention of staking a claim to the throne. He is a farmer and local councillor in an Australian town who moved to Australia when he was 18. So, do we have an imposter on the throne? On studying his family tree, have we missed out on Queen Barbara I, King Henry IX, King Theophilus II, and the current King Michael I?

To conclude, and food for thought if you think this illegitimate line has put an imposter on the throne, do you really think there were no other illegitimate children born to 'other' fathers during the last thousand years of royal procreation? Do you really think every queen has remained faithful and every king has only ever brought up his own biological children? Figures in the Twenty-First Century suggest something like one in five men bring up a child they think is their own. Surely this has happened in the royal line of descent too.

Others might be quick to point out that the House of Windsor, the Hanoverians and the House of Orange, for example, were all natural imposters in the natural line of succession. James II of England and Ireland (VII of Scotland) and his descendants are the natural heirs to the throne. James reigned from 1685 for just over three years. He was seen as too Catholic, too pro-French and too absolutist. There is an argument that he was a popular man, but his policies were just too unpopular. The English Parliament plotted against him and brought over his son-in-law William Prince of Orange (a Dutch Stadtholder) to regain control and stop James putting Catholics in high places throughout the kingdom. But James fled to France and William was offered the Crown. Jacobites (James's supporters) claimed James was the true king and tried to invade from Ireland with the help of the King of France Louis XIV; they failed. There were several attempts, but William, now William III of England, and King of Scotland and Ireland was not firmly on the throne. If you trace the Stuart line (James's royal house) through the nobility and sovereigns of Europe, you will come out through the Bavarian and Liechtenstein lines, and eventually Prince Alois and Joespeh Wenzel, born in the 1990s. Jacobites would argue that this family line hold a better claim to the British crown than Elizabeth II.

ROYAL SCANDALS SET IN RHYME

Today royal scandals are usually well documented in the newspapers, told on the television and radio, discussed on the internet, and written about in books! But hundreds of years ago, these stories were told in a different way. Of course there was gossip, books and print, but literacy rates were poor. Most people could not read and write properly, many were uneducated. As a nightmare for historians, stories passed down through word of mouth, which could dramatically change. However, nursery rhymes have unwittingly preserved many events in history, from the bubonic plague in A Ring a Ring a Roses, to the English Civil War in Humpty Dumpty. So, with the majority of people illiterate at that time, singing or chanting a rhyme would help them remember and pass on scandals, gossip and stories of royalty and history to their friends and more importantly, their children and grandchildren.

Of course nursery rhymes are not accurate historical facts per se, and one has to consider exaggeration and the story-telling factor, but they do give us an insight into some of the battles, scandals, feelings of the people, affairs, diseases and political controversies; with some facts to consider. They should be taken more as entertainment than historical fact, but at the same time we should not underestimate the amount of information presented in each one. The other problem is some have more than one explanation and story behind them. Here

And Finally Did You Know . . .

I have picked a handful of nursery rhymes and have generally tried to present the most popular explanation into what the rhyme is about. This is a big subject in its own right and I have just given it a brief mention to show how scandal and history have been set in rhyme.

BAA BAA BLACK SHEEP

Baa baa black sheep, have you any wool?
Yes sir, yes sir, three bags full!
One for the master, one for the dame,
And one for the little boy who lives down the lane.

England's critical wool industry is celebrated in this rhyme. It has been suggested the rhyme was a dig at King Edward I and the export tax he imposed, allowing him to collect tax on any wool exports from any port in the country. It does not sound much of a scandal now, but back then it really was a big deal, a scandalous tax!

OLD MOTHER HUBBARD

Old Mother Hubbard
Went to the cupboard
To get her poor doggie a bone.
When she got there
The cupboard was bare
So the poor little doggie had none.

This rhyme refers to King Henry VIII's chief minister Cardinal Wolsey and his unsuccessful attempts to get King Henry VIII's marriage to Catherine of Aragon annulled by the Catholic Church in Rome. Wolsey is supposed to be Old Mother Hubbard, going to the cupboard (Church) to get a bone for the doggie (an annulment for the King).

MARY MARY QUITE CONTRARY

Mary Mary quite contrary
How does your garden grow?
With silver bells and cockle shells
And pretty maids all in a row.

This refers to Mary I (Bloody Mary), and the garden is supposed to be the graveyards filling up with all the Protestants she had executed.

The silver bells and cockle shells were nicknames for torture devices. The bells crushed thumbs and the cockleshells were thought to refer to torture devices designed to attach to genitals and cause excruciating pain. The maids, (maiden) was a guillotine device.

PUSSYCAT PUSSYCAT, WHERE HAVE YOU BEEN?

"Pussycat pussycat, where have you been?"
"I've been to London to see the Queen."
"Pussycat pussycat, what did you dare?"
"I frightened a little mouse under her chair."

This tells the story of one of the lady's-in-waiting to Elizabeth I. The servant let her old cat wander round Windsor Castle. The animal is supposed to have walked under the Queen's chair and scared her witless as its tail gently brushed against her. Elizabeth allowed the cat to stay, as long as it kept mice away from her, as part of the deal.

GEORGIE PORGIE PUDDING AND PIE

Georgie Porgie pudding and pie,
Kissed the girls and made them cry.
When the boys came out to play,
Georgie Porgie ran away.

This refers to the courtier George Villiers, the lover of King James I. But the dashing young man was also admired by the ladies! He had an affair with Anne of Austria who was Queen of France and married to the French King Louis XIII. Villiers helped arrange the marriage of King James's son (later Charles I) to the French Princess Henrietta Maria, who was a Catholic. The scandal of his affairs and his support of the marriage of Charles, made him many enemies in the country.

JACK AND JILL

Jack and Jill went up the hill to fetch a pail of water
Jack fell down and broke his crown
And Jill came tumbling after.
Up got Jack, and home did trot
As fast as he could caper
He went to bed and bound his head
With vinegar and brown paper.

And Finally Did You Know . . .

This tells the story of King Louis XVI (Jack) who was beheaded (lost his crown) followed by his Queen Marie Antoinette (Jill). The beheadings happened during the Reign of Terror in 1793. It is thought the happy ending was added later.

JACK SPRAT

Jack Sprat could eat no fat
His wife could eat no lean,
And so betwixt the two of them
They licked the platter clean.
Jack ate all the lean
Joan ate all the fat,
The bone they picked it clean
Then gave it to the cat.
Jack Sprat was wheeling
His wife by the ditch.
The barrow turned over
And in she did pitch.
Says Jack, "She'll be drowned!"
But Joan did reply,
"I don't think I shall
For the ditch is quite dry."

There are several possible backgrounds to this well-known nursery rhyme. The first being that Jack Sprat is really King Charles I (1625–1649) and Henrietta Maria, his Queen (1609–1669). Apparently, when King Charles (Jack Sprat) declared war on Spain, Parliament refused to finance him (leaving him lean)! So his wife imposed an illegal war tax (to get some fat), after the angered King (Jack Sprat) dissolved Parliament.

It is also suggested that Jack Sprat tells the intriguing story of King Richard I (Richard the Lionheart) (1157–1199) and his brother King John (1167–1216), their internal squabbles over the throne, John's greedy wife Joan, Richard being taken hostage abroad and the ransom, once paid, keeping England financially destitute for years.

LITTLE JACK HORNER

Little Jack Horner sat in the corner
Eating his Christmas pie,
He put in his thumb and pulled out a plum
And said "What a good boy am I!"

This strange rhyme is supposed to deal with the Bishop of Glastonbury 1461–1539, and his attempts to bribe King Henry VIII not to take his Abbey and lands, one of the wealthiest in the country at that time. During the Dissolution of the Monasteries, and the stealing of their treasures and selling off of their lands, the Bishop put the deeds to 12 estates in a pie. The Bishop sent his Steward Thomas Horner to London with the pie, but apparently Horner opened the pie and picked the deeds to a manor called Mells (the prize plum of the 12) and kept it for himself. The Bishop was executed for treason, by being hung, drawn and quartered at Glastonbury. Horner moved into Mells and the Horner family owned the property until the Twentieth Century. His descendants claim they paid for the manor and the rhyme is untrue.

GOOSEY GOOSEY GANDER

Goosey Goosey Gander where shall I wander,
Upstairs, downstairs and in my lady's chamber.
There I met an old man who wouldn't say his prayers,
I took him by the left leg and threw him down the stairs.

This dates back to the early 1500s, when Catholic priests had to hide in priest holes to escape Protestants who were against Catholicism. Those caught hiding, along with the family helping them, were usually executed. The rhyme tells the scandalous story of religious persecution during the Reformation, under King Henry VIII. The rhyme suggests something bad may happen to those forgetting to say their Protestant prayers in the proper English tongue, rather than the old Catholic prayers that were usually said in Latin.

And Finally Did You Know . . .

OLD KING COLE

Old King Cole was a merry old soul, and a merry old soul
    was he,
He called for his pipe in the middle of the night
And he called for his fiddlers three.
Every fiddler had a fine fiddle, and a very fine fiddle had he,
Oh there's none so rare as can compare
With King Cole and his fiddlers three.

This rhyme is hundreds of years old, dating as far back as the Third Century BC. It is unclear exactly who Old King Cole was, or what the story was really about. There are several possible contenders for the identity of King Cole, from the Third and Fourth Century AD.

The story either celebrates the history of the Ancient Britons or was a kind of political broadcast of its day, used later by the Tudor dynasty who claimed to descend from Old King Cole's royal lineage. Thus, this tale attempts to legitimise the Tudor's claim to the throne. The four contenders for Old King Cole are Coel Godhebog born 220 (Decurion of Rome), Coel Hen born 350 AD, St Ceneu ap Coel born 382 AD and the rather strange suggestion of Richard Cole-brook, a Reading clothier a few hundred years later!

THE QUEEN OF HEARTS

The Queen of Hearts she made some tarts all on a summer's day,
The Knave of Hearts he stole the tarts and took them clean away.
The King of Hearts called for the tarts and beat the Knave full
    score.
The Knave of Hearts brought back the tarts and
vowed he'd steal no more.

The exact history of this rhyme is unclear. But some historians believe it is about Elizabeth of Bohemia, of Scottish birth and daughter of King James VI. Her brother was Charles I. She was a Scottish Princess, but also Queen of Bohemia for a few months. She was very popular with the people and nicknamed Queen of Hearts, just as Diana, Princess of Wales became known. The rhyme first appeared in 1782 and again in *Alice in Wonderland* in 1805.

STRANGE FACTS ABOUT ROYALS

- King Louis XIV of France only took three baths in his whole life
- Pharaoh Pepi II of Egypt had the longest known reign of any monarch (94 years)
- Queen Victoria survived seven assassination attempts
- Queen Elizabeth II and the Duke of Edinburgh have sent about 37,500 Christmas cards during her reign
- The shortest reigning English monarch was Lady Jane Grey who ruled for nine days in 1553; some count it as 13 days (never crowned)
- 'Queen' (Empress) Matilda (never crowned and only temporarily took over) was only 4'2" in height, making her England's shortest ever monarch
- King Alexandros I of Greece died in 1920 after being bitten by his pet monkey. He got blood poisoning
- King Henry VI came to the Throne in 1422 aged just nine months
- The first Prime Minister that Queen Elizabeth met who had been born during her reign, was Tony Blair
- Queen Elizabeth II is descended from Cerdic, the early Sixth Century King of the West Saxons
- Elizabeth of York, wife of King Henry VII, is the Queen of hearts on a pack of playing cards. It was his romantic idea to create something for people to admire
- Only two English monarchs have reigned more than once – King Henry VI and King Edward IV
- The fourth Moghul Emperor, Jahangir, who reigned 1605 to 1627, had 300 wives, 5,000 extra women, and 1,000 young men for a bit of variety!
- The remains of Henry VIII's Palace of Oatlands are underneath the foundations of a Weybridge Council estate in Surrey
- In 2002 at 76 years of age Queen Elizabeth II was the oldest monarch to celebrate a Golden Jubilee
- Prince Naruhito of Japan went to Oxford University but had to be shown how to iron his shirt, by his police escort
- Queen Elizabeth II sent her first email in 1976 from an Army base
- It's reported that the film *The Madness of King George* was originally called 'The Madness of George III'. But it was feared Americans would wonder where films I and II had gone
- Victoria is the longest reigning monarch of Great Britain so far, at 63 years

- Prince Andrew was the first child to be born to a reigning monarch (Queen Elizabeth II) for 103 years

IN CONCLUSION

'the office of the king in this nation is unnecessary, burdensome and dangerous to the liberty, society and public interest of the people.'

(Parliamentary statement after the execution of King Charles I in 1649)

For many years there has been a call to end the monarchy in this country. Its existence has been called into question a number of times. I always thought the most convincing argument for keeping the monarchy was to show how it attracted so many visitors to Great Britain, and how that must be good for the economy. That argument was all but killed off by Nick Margerrison, a late night talk-show host on London's LBC Radio. When discussing this topic with listeners, he claimed the Palace of Versailles has more visitors per year than Buckingham Palace, and how long is it since France had a royal family? This made me think, does any country actually need a monarchy to attract tourists? People flock to France to see the Eiffel tower and others visit Moscow's Red Square. Meanwhile people flock to places as diverse as Disneyland, Times Square, Alton Towers, Niagara Falls and the Cotswolds, without royal connections. Ask yourself, would people come to Britain to see Windsor Castle and Buckingham Palace even if the royal family was no more? Would they come and see where the royals used to live and work? And here is a question just as important: is the monarchy capable of killing itself off through scandal, bad reputation, greed, being generally superfluous, or any combination of the above.

In Europe today there are fewer than a dozen monarchies left, including Belgium, Denmark, United Kingdom, Liechtenstein, Monaco, The Netherlands, Norway, Spain and Sweden. Technically, although not counted here, The Vatican City is a monarchy and Luxembourg is an independent Grand Duchy. In Geoffrey Hindley's *The Royal Families of Europe*, he says many of the Continent's monarchs survived things like revolution, warfare, regicides and their own incompetence. Many countries or principalities have got rid of their monarchy, duchy or empire title and become a republic such as

Albania, Austria-Hungary, Bavaria, Germany, Brunswick, Iceland, Italy, Lippe, Montenegro, Oldenburg, Prussia, Romania, Serbia, Yugoslavia and Portugal. Spain got rid of its monarchy and then restored it.

How far has the monarchy developed since 1901, and is it capable of moving with the times? Also, how has it coped with, and been judged by, the scandal that surrounds it. Since the age of the first monarchs in this country, as far back as 600 AD, each one has had to fight for their survival, power and recognition. As the centuries rolled on, kings and queens continued to fight and battle, or change and develop, in the interests of stability and succession. A thousand years ago, the battlefield was a more likely arena for a monarch to express their authority.

But the monarchy has changed, and arguably kept in step, usually, with society at large; a monarch no longer fends off tribes of barbarians, executes those out of favour, or commands a British Empire. The monarchy now has a different place. The Nineteenth Century writer Walter Bagehot said the Sovereign has the right to be consulted, to encourage and to warn. He argues that a king of any great sagacity would want nothing else. As we examined in the introduction of this book, over the last one hundred years or so, in Europe, the royal landscape has greatly changed. In 1914, at the start of World War I, Europe was mostly ruled by royalty. By 1939, the political picture was rather different; most countries in Europe had become republics. John Cannon, *Survival of the British Monarchy*, argues it is a minority taste, with fewer than 10 per cent of the world's population being 'subjects' of a monarchy: Britons, Australians, Dutch, Japanese, Moroccans, Nepalese, Jordanians, Canadians, Danes, Spaniards and Swedes, being the best examples.

Some countries have abandoned their monarchy after losing wars and undergoing profound social and political change. But Britain's victory in two world wars has helped secure the country's independence, stability and sovereignty. Britain's monarchy has reinvented itself many times and adapted to change. In modern times it is further removed from politics than ever, and that has done the office of the Sovereign nothing but good. Also, Britain's monarchy is international; a remnant of the British Empire. But it has adapted and changed with the times over the last hundred years or so. It is fair to argue that some of the most subtle, and biggest, changes, have come since the death of Queen Victoria in 1901.

And Finally Did You Know . . .

Let us look at each monarch since 1901 and determine the changes he or she has made, as a way of reinventing 'the firm', as well as looking at the overall picture since 1901. Royal watcher Robert Hardman says the monarchy has to adapt and modernise. He states the Queen made that clear in 1997 after the royal family misjudged the mood of the nation in the aftermath of Diana's death. Some referred to the Queen's error as a major scandal of the day.

The Queen, whether or not seeing it as a scandal, acknowledges that the survival of royalty depends on public support. During a luncheon to celebrate her Golden Wedding anniversary she told the then Prime Minister Tony Blair that he was chosen through the ballot box but the royal family has to listen to public opinion, which is often harder to read and understand. Blair said at that time the monarchy was the best way to keep the country together during a changing world.

For hundreds of years there has been a threat of republicanism in Britain. Andrjez Olechnowicz reminds us in *The Monarchy and the British Nation* that Tennyson called this country a 'crown'd republic'. Bagehot referred to it as 'a disguised republic'. The Queen's former top courtier, the Lord Chamberlain, Lord Luce, once said that the monarchy's very survival depends on popular support and adapting rather than just existing.

The republican movement has existed for hundreds of years, reaching its peak when King Charles I was executed in 1649. However, according to a 2010 poll, 76 per cent of those questioned said the monarchy should continue after the Queen dies, 18 per cent wanted a republic; almost one-in-five people. There are regular polls on this, by many different pollsters, and the results differ widely. But Billig notes in *Talking of the Royal Family* that it is interesting no main political party calls for a republic, instead letting the fringe Marxist groups tackle the issue. He notes how even the republicans in Northern Ireland do not campaign for general republicanism.

The royals have always survived scandal; it does not seem to be the ingredient that causes its downfall. The monarchy always benefits from sympathy though. Two notable examples are the Prince of Wales getting typhoid in 1870 and the death of Diana, Princess of Wales, in 1997. Polls often show an increase in favour of the royals and a fall in any feelings of republicanism.

One could argue the case that the British monarchy felt it needed to reconstruct itself after Queen Victoria had kept herself to herself for so long. King Edward VII (reigned 1901–1910) had the responsibility for bringing back the family into the public domain. But with the rise of socialism, Kier Hardy and the Labour movement, the monarchy faced a potential left wing threat. If remaining politically detached has been a recipe for survival Frank Prochaska notes in *The Republic of Britain* that Edward's inclination to interfere in politics less than his mother Queen Victoria meant that he gave little ammunition to his enemies. He suggests Edward's different style, of keeping quiet on state affairs, unlike Victoria, kept the mood of republicanism at bay. Edward continued changes initiated by his mother aimed at distancing the family from the days of the scandalous and glutinous King George IV. Prochaska argues that the family now held more than a thousand patronages, mainly helping the poor, with a momentous shift in their endeavours, reaching throughout the country, courting good publicity and thereby adjusting to a new style democracy in the country. It is charity work that we now commonly associate the royal family within the Twenty-First Century. The royals have become more aware of public opinion, and today's Prince of Wales is not associated with the scandalous, fast-living, high-spending, partying mode of those before him. Although one could argue there was enough scandal linked to his first marriage to keep him going for a life time.

In 2005, royal watcher Richard Fitz-Williams, in defence of public feeling against Charles's marriage to Camilla, told CNN that the Prince had made a popularity comeback because of his unwavering charity work. He suggested the job of Prince of Wales is a difficult one. He said people were more than happy to give Charles a second chance, rather than him be stuck in an impossible role. He described the post of Prince of Wales as a predicament rather than a position. On scandal he was quick to point out nobody was around to chronicle the playboy and libertine behaviours of former Prince of Wales's, like they have been for Charles Windsor, watching his every movement. John Cannon claims, in *Survival of the British Monarchy*, the more freedom we get, the more standards we expect of our royal family.

King George V reigned from 1910 to 1936. Before becoming King, George V started a series of goodwill tours to mining and industrial areas, taking royalty to the working classes of the country. This was a new policy for the monarchy. In addition, King George V was fortunate in that he could address a nation through the new medium of radio. The monarchy embraced this new technology and this was one of the biggest changes. Arguably the biggest reinvention made by the monarchy for some years was George V changing the name of the royal house, from Saxe-Coburg and Gotha to the House of Windsor. He did this during World War I, to rid the family of all German names and titles. If the monarchy had remained 'German' during World War II, it may have been a scandal too far for its survival. This was proof that change and reinvention was a crucial ingredient to survival. The name change was crucial. The British monarchy had to evolve so it could survive.

George V also saw the need to change the way the monarch ruled overseas. It was under this kingship that the Statute of Westminster separated the crown. Dominions became separate kingdoms, leading the way to colonial independence and the beginning of the end of the Empire and birth of the Commonwealth. The reinvention of its leadership and the building blocks for the Commonwealth was an important part of the royal family reinventing itself in the Twentieth Century.

King Edward VIII reigned in 1936, becoming King after George V died. He abdicated because of a constitutional crisis regarding his relationship with Wallis Simpson, an American divorcee. Perhaps this is a perfect example of the monarchy reinventing itself, listening to opposition, putting the country first and being a considerate monarch. After all, one could argue this was the biggest scandal ever to hit the monarchy. Edward's special admiration of the Nazis added to this scandal. But to abdicate, marry Simpson and pave the way for his brother George VI to be crowned, was surely the ultimate sacrifice. The royal family survived the crisis and reinvented itself by replacing Edward with George VI.

John Wheeler Bennett's 1958 authorised biography *King George VI: His Life and Reign* praised the King, for developing a new concept of royalty, closely identified with the people and genuinely interested in their affairs. This is a pattern of reinvention apparent and recurrent in the House of Windsor. King George VI and his wife Queen Elizabeth toured Britain's bombed cities during World War II. Even Buckingham Palace was bombed and Elizabeth said on one visit to a bomb site that she was glad the royals had been bombed because it made her feel she could look the East End in the face.

Queen Elizabeth II (reigned 1952-present) could become Britain's longest ever serving monarch, beating Queen Victoria's 63 years. There is evidence that under Elizabeth II, the royal family has changed and reinvented itself more than at any other time in history.

There is also an argument there has been more scandal than at any other time. One could argue though, that it has just been better documented because of the modern day media. Here was the first ever televised coronation and the first televised Christmas message. Television, radio, newspapers and magazines thrust the royal family into the public eye more than ever before, although the first palace press officer was actually employed in 1918. Queen Elizabeth II has presided over a massive expansion of press personnel at the palace. The royals have offered press releases and organised photo opportunities. From my own experience royal press officers can be obstructive and not terribly forthcoming with information. One has to ask whether this irresponsible behaviour has encouraged the more unscrupulous tabloid style journalists, to fill in a few blanks during times of scandal and crisis.

The internet has forced the royal family to reinvent itself again and move with the times. The monarchy has again embraced this development and turned it to its own advantage. There is an official royal family website and the Queen's Christmas speech is put online, on its own site and on *youtube.com* as well. The British monarch's head has always been embossed on our currency. This is a tradition that can be found as far back as Anglo-Saxon coinage.

When Tony Benn, the former MP and Postmaster General, approached the Queen to suggest her head be taken off some stamps, she refused. But Benn did get the Queen to at least look at alternative designs. Now there are plenty of stamps without the monarch's head.

Today, royal finances are a big issue. The monarchy has been economising for some years, paying tax, making various cut backs. The royals are far more aware of public feeling over this than ever before. They have undergone a huge amount of streamlining. Palace accountants now keep a tight grip on expenditure.

In Antony Taylor's anti-monarchy *Down with the Crown* he says that most reformers have been happy with cosmetic tinkering of the excesses: discarding the Royal Yacht Britannia or cutting down the number of minor royals getting Civil List pensions. In 2009, changes were being put forward to modernise the royal family. In the *Daily Mail*'s article 'Fiddling with the Monarchy while Britain Burns', 28 March 2009, it said a Private Member's Bill in Parliament had been put forward in an attempt to remove the ban on a monarch marrying a Roman Catholic and the ancient practice of primogeniture. At the time Prime Minister Gordon Brown said the 1701 Act of Succession which outlines the rules, must be removed. The article said he described primogeniture, where male heirs take favour over female heirs, as discriminatory although the article's author Peter McKay gave it the 'burning' title hinting that changing the monarchy whilst suffering a recession, should be a low priority. Recently Prince Charles hinted he wanted to become 'defender of faiths', not 'the faith', recognising Britain's diversity. Some people argued that this was a scandalous comment, further chipping away as Britain's Christian history.

If you look at the autocratic dominance of previous hard line monarchs such as King Henry VIII, Queen Mary I and William the Conqueror, for example, and compare it to today's royal family appearing in *It's a Royal Knockout* on television, it shows how the royals have tried to show their friendly side, and be one of us!

Writer John Cannon argues the Twentieth Century saw a big change in the functions of the monarchy, claiming the royals are now at the heart of a diverse and multi-cultural Commonwealth, as opposed to the old Empire. He is also quick to point out the monarchy has stripped itself of many of its old prerogatives; in practice relinquishing power and responsibility. The calls for the UK to become a republic are ongoing. Other countries too have campaigned for an end to the monarchy. The 'Common Cause' is an alliance of republican movements within the Commonwealth of Nations. 'The monarchy is damaging to those caught up in it, it is unaccountable and it acts as a drag on our democratic process,' says the website *republic.org*. Arguments against having a royal family include; religious discrimination, sexism, non-impartiality, cost and the fact one is expected to bow to them. But many in favour of our royal family (the clear majority), despite the problems and scandal, argue they provide a safeguard against government instability, offer value for money, promotion and patronage of charities, promotion of British business abroad and leadership and support to the armed forces.

The royals have given us scandal after scandal, but nevertheless, Elizabeth II is expected to become the longest serving monarch in British history. The scandals have been balanced out with healthy changes in this current reign alone. There is a televised Christmas speech to the nation, the State opening of Parliament is on live TV, the palace is open to the public, the Queen pays taxes, the civil list has shrunk, and there have been pop concerts at the palace; even Queen's guitarist Brian May stood on the roof of Buckingham Palace to play *God Save the Queen* during the Golden Jubilee celebrations in

2002. If that is not moving with the times, then I do not know what is! The monarchy has always reinvented itself, either by evolving or careful planning. It is a fair view and solid argument that both are especially true since 1901. And on this subject, Robert Hardman in *The Royal Family at Work* quotes the classic novel *The Leopard* and the well-known line in it that says, 'If we want things to stay the same, things will have to change'.

AN AFTERTHOUGHT: WHY HISTORY LESSONS ARE IMPORTANT

History lessons in schools are fading fast. Once compulsory throughout senior schools, now some children are allowed to drop history at the age of 13. Where will it end? No history lessons in schools at all? We will get to the stage where your children or grand-children will have no idea who Queen Victoria, or President Kennedy was. They will be unaware of historical milestones like the Battle of Hastings in 1066 and the dates of the two world wars. Politicians have already realised their previous poor attitudes to lessons such as PE and cookery; vital life skills subjects. They will eventually realise their mistakes over history lessons, when our descendants become the dunces of the world.

To prove my point, in a recent survey almost one in ten school children thought the Queen invented the telephone, and not Alexander Graham Bell. Four per cent actually thought Noel Edmonds invented the telephone because of his TV programme *Deal or No Deal*. Many thought Buzz Lightyear, from Disney blockbuster *Toy Story*, was the first man on the moon, instead of Neil Armstrong. Some youngsters thought Luke Skywalker made 'one giant leap for mankind' instead of Armstrong. Where will it all end?

Bibliography

REFERENCE BOOKS

Alexander, J.T., *Catherine the Great: Life and Legend*, Oxford University Press, 1989

Billig, M., *Talking of the Royal Family*, Routledge, London, 1998

Campbell, B., *Princess of Wales, How Sexual Politics Shook the Monarchy*, Women's Press, 1998

Cannon, J., *The Survival of the British Monarchy*, RHS 5th Series, 1986

Cawthorne, N., *Royal Scandals*, Chancellor Press, London, 1999

Cocks, H., *Advances in the Modern History of Sexuality*, Palgrave Macmillan, 2006

Cohen, W.A., *Sex Scandal: The Private Parts of Victorian Fiction*, Duke University Press, 1996

Doran, S., *Monarchy and Matrimony: The Courtships of Elizabeth I*, Routledge, London, 1996

Eddcardt, T., *Secrets of the Seven Smallest States of Europe: Andorra, Liechtenstein, Luxembourg, Malta, Monaco, San Marino and Vatican City*, Hippocrene Books Inc. USA, 2005

Edwards, A., *The Grimaldis of Monaco: Centuries of Scandal, Years of Grace*, Harper Collins, London, 1992

Farquhar, M., *A Treasury of Royal Scandals*, Penguin Books, London, 2001

Haigh, C., *Elizabeth I*, Longman, London, 1988

Hardman, R., *Monarchy: The Royal Family at Work*, Ebury Press, London, 2007

Haslip, J., *Catherine the Great*, Weidenfield and Nicolson, London, 1977

Havers, M., (Rt Hon), Grayson, E. and Shankland, P., *Royal Baccarat Scandal (The)*, Souvenir Press, 1977

Hibbert, C., *Edward VII*, Palgrave, 2007

Hindley, G., *The Royal Families of Europe*, Carroll & Graf Inc., 2000

Hoak, D., & Feingold, M., *The World of William & Mary*, Stanford University Press, California, 1996

Holmes, G., (ed.), *Britain After the Glorious Revolution, 1689–1714*, Macmillan London, 1969

King, J., and Beveridge, J., *Diana: the Evidence*, Previewed on Google Books, S.P. Books, Inc., 2007

Lee, S., *Queen Victoria A Biography*, John Murray, London, 1902

Marshall, R.K., *Elizabeth I*, MSO London, in association with the National Portrait Gallery, 1991

Mijers, E., & Onnekink, D., (eds.), *The Impact of the King Stad-Holder in International Context*, Ashgate Publishing Ltd. Aldershot, 2007

Olechnowicz, A., *The Monarchy and the British Nation 1780–Present Day*, Cambridge University Press (via Google Books), 2007

Osen, D., *Royal Scandals, True Tales of Sex, Lust and Greed, Friedman*, Fairfax Publishers, New York, 1995

Paxman, J., *On Royalty*, Viking/Penguin London, 2006

Prochaska, F., *The Republic of Britain*, Penguin Books, London, 2000

Raeff, M., *Catherine the Great*, Hill and Wang, New York, 1972

Smith, E.A., *A Queen On Trial, The Affair of Queen Caroline*, Alan Sutton Publishing, Stroud, 1993

Somerset-Fry, P., , Dorling Kindersley, London, 1996

Taylor, A., *Down with the Crown*, Reaktion Books, 1999

Weir, A., Children of England: *The Heirs of King Henry VIII*, Pimlico, London, 1997

Wilkinson, J., *Mary Boleyn: The True Story of Henry VIII's Mistress*, Amberley Publishing, 2009

WEBSITES

abebookes.com
alfayed.com
allsands.com/history
Bambooweb.com
bbc.co.uk/history/british/tudors/Elizabeth
bbc.co.uk/news
bertha-lum.org
britannia.com/history/monarchs
british-history.ac.uk
ceridian.co.uk/Daily Telegraph
Channel4.com/history

Bibliography

channel4.com/history

eebo.chadwyck.com

elizabethi.org

englishmonarchs.co.uk

essortment.com

fordham.edu/halsall/mod/elizabeth1

Foxnews.com article, Scientists: Incest Doomed European Dynasty, by Andrea Thompson, (published April 16th, 2009)

geo.ed.ac.uk/scotgaz

geo.ed.ac.uk/scotgaz

Glbtq.com

helium.com/debates

highlanderweb.co.uk

historyhome.co.uk

hrp.org

http://hansardmillbanksystems.com/lords

http://transcripts.cnn.com/TRANSCRIPTS/0502/10/lol.05.html

http://www.sentex.net/~ajy/facts/monarchs.html

imdb.com

irishtimes.com

irishtimes.com

japanexplained.wordpress.com/japanese

leninports.com

merryroyals.com

nydailynews.com

reuters.com

rhymes.org.uk

southcoasttoday.com

spartacus.schoolnet.co.uk

The Irish National Caucus and Peace Foundation website, December 2009

thehistorylearningsite.co.uk

thepeerage.com

tudors.org

www.britannica.com

www.east-ayrshire.gov.uk

www.eebo.chadwyck.com

www.encyclopedia.com/topic/ActofSettlement

www.irishnationalcaucus.org/pages/Articles2004/TheOrangeOrder .htm

www.manchestereveningnews.co.uk/news/
www.mnsu.edu/emuseum/
www.msu.edu
www.nydailynews.com/archives
www.royal.gov.uk/home
www.rusticgirls.com/family/royalty
www.undiscoveredscotland.co.uk
youtube.com/britainsrealmonarch

TV, RADIO AND NEWSPAPERS

Channel 4
Dailymail.co.uk
foxnews.com
GMTV archive interview
Independent (The), Dynasty that dominated Europe for more than 500 years was undone by incest, by Steve Connor, April 15th 2009
Majesty Magazine, Rex Publications, London, interview with Joe Little, Managing Editor March 2009.
Sky.com/news
Star FM, interview with former reporter covering Windsor Castle, Michael Barry, March 2009
Telegraph in 2003 by Christopher Howse
TES Magazine, Published in London, 1998
The Times newspaper
yorkshirepost.co.uk
The Daily Mail Newspaper 28 March 2009, Peter McKay
Telegraph.co.uk By Fiona Govan in Madrid Published 15 Apr 2009
Mail on Sunday Aug 23, 2009, Miles Goslett
Milwaukee Sentinel, Dec 28, 1962, accessed via news.google.com /newspapers

Index

Index

Index